200+

chess puzzles

puzzles d'échecs

rompecabezas de ajedrez

Schachrätsel

łamigłówki szachowe

schaak puzzels

ŝakenigmoj

Bibliographische Information der Deutschen Bibliothek:
Die Deutsche Bibliothek verzeichnet diese Publikation in der Deutschen
Nationalbibliographie; detaillierte bibliographische Daten sind im Internet über
http://dnb.ddb.de abrufbar.

Bibliographic information from the Deutsche Bibliothek: The Deutsche Bibliothek lists this
publication in the Deutsche Nationalbibliographie; detailed bibliographic data can be accessed
on the Internet at http://dnb.ddb.de.

Informations bibliographiques de la Deutsche Bibliothek: La Deutsche Bibliothek répertorie
cette publication dans la Deutsche Nationalbibliographie ; des données bibliographiques
détaillées peuvent être consultées sur Internet à l'adresse http://dnb.ddb.de.

Información bibliográfica de la Deutsche Bibliothek: La Deutsche Bibliothek incluye esta
publicación en la Deutsche Nationalbibliographie; Se puede acceder a datos bibliográficos
detallados en Internet en http://dnb.ddb.de.

Informacje bibliograficzne z Deutsche Bibliothek: Deutsche Bibliothek wymienia tę publikację w
Deutsche Nationalbibliographie; szczegółowe dane bibliograficzne można znaleźć w Internecie
pod adresem http://dnb.ddb.de.

Bibliografische informatie van de Deutsche Bibliothek: De Deutsche Bibliothek vermeldt deze
publicatie in de Deutsche Nationalbibliographie; gedetailleerde bibliografische gegevens
kunnen op internet worden geraadpleegd op http://dnb.ddb.de.

Bibliografiaj informoj de la Deutsche Bibliothek: La Deutsche Bibliothek listigas ĉi tiun
publikaĵon en la Deutsche Nationalbibliographie; detalaj bibliografiaj datumoj estas alireblaj en
la Interreto ĉe http://dnb.ddb.de.

Herstellung und Verlag: BoD – Books on Demand, Norderstedt
ISBN: 978-3-756-25892-5

Opening

About this book

On the following pages you will find over 200 chess problems that will end in checkmate in just a few moves. The puzzles are based on realistic game situations and are divided into chapters. The solutions start on page (🔆⇨) 74. A small circle at the bottom right of each diagram indicates which color you are playing and it is your turn. The notation of the solutions corresponds approximately to the international shorthand algebraic notation. The moves are numbered from the situation shown, in addition an asterisk (*) has been introduced, which marks any legal move. Alternative solutions were also occasionally given. A completeness and correctness of the solutions is not guaranteed.

Forsyth-Edwards notation as QR codes

Forsyth-Edwards Notations (FEN) of all puzzles are provided as QR codes at the end of this book. This allows you to load the starting position of each puzzle into any chess app that supports the FEN simply by scanning the given code. The solutions are not included in the QR codes.

Tips for use

It is of course up to you how you solve the puzzles in this book. Nonetheless, I would like to offer you a few suggestions that may improve the "user experience".

- **Don't go in order**
  If you regularly look at the solutions (to verify a found solution or to look up a solution of an unsolved puzzle), then do not go through the puzzles in order. You look too quickly at the neighboring solutions and accidentally might take the first move or even the entire solution of the next puzzle with you.

- **Solve the puzzles on a real board**
  It is of course a matter of taste, but I personally find it more pleasant to set up the game situation on a real board, especially since solving a position on a board also trains the spatial perception of pieces and their attack angles enormously.

- **Play both sides**
  Especially with the "longer" problems, a checkmate is often possible in fewer moves if countermoves are not forced and the opposing side reacts unwisely. Always try to find the best possible move for the opponent to extend the game.

Ouverture

À propos de ce livre

Dans les pages suivantes, vous trouverez plus de 200 problèmes d'échecs qui se terminent par un échec et mat en quelques coups seulement. Les puzzles sont basés sur des situations de jeu réalistes et sont divisés en chapitres. Les solutions commencent à la page 74. Un petit cercle en bas à droite de chaque diagramme indique la couleur que vous jouez et c'est votre tour. La notation des solutions correspond approximativement à la notation algébrique abrégée internationale. Les coups sont numérotés à partir de la situation indiquée, en plus un astérisque (*) a été introduit, qui marque tout coup légal. Des solutions alternatives ont aussi parfois été proposées. L'exhaustivité et l'exactitude des solutions ne sont pas garanties.

FEN sous forme de codes QR

Les notations Forsyth-Edwards (FEN) de tous les puzzles sont fournies sous forme de codes QR à la fin de ce livre. Cela vous permet de charger la position de départ de chaque puzzle dans n'importe quelle application d'échecs prenant en charge le FEN simplement en scannant le code donné. Les solutions ne sont pas incluses dans les codes QR.

Conseils d'utilisation

C'est bien sûr à vous de décider comment résoudre les énigmes de ce livre. Néanmoins, je voudrais vous proposer quelques suggestions susceptibles d'améliorer "l'expérience utilisateur".

- **Ne va pas dans l'ordre**

  Si vous consultez régulièrement les solutions (pour vérifier une solution trouvée ou pour rechercher la solution d'un puzzle non résolu), ne parcourez pas les puzzles dans l'ordre. Vous regardez trop rapidement les solutions voisines et vous pourriez accidentellement prendre le premier pas ou même la solution entière du puzzle suivant avec vous.

- **Résolvez les énigmes sur un vrai échiquier**

  C'est bien sûr une question de goût, mais personnellement je trouve plus agréable de mettre en place la situation de jeu sur un vrai échiquier, d'autant que résoudre une position sur un échiquier entraîne aussi énormément la perception spatiale des pièces et leurs angles d'attaque.

- **Jouez les deux contreparties**

  Surtout avec les problèmes "plus longs", un échec et mat est souvent possible en moins de coups si les contre-mouvements ne sont pas forcés et que le camp adverse réagit de manière imprudente. Essayez toujours de trouver le meilleur coup possible pour l'adversaire afin de prolonger le jeu.

Apertura

Sobre este libro

En las siguientes páginas encontrará más de 200 problemas de ajedrez que terminarán en jaque mate en tan solo unos pocos movimientos. Los rompecabezas se basan en situaciones de juego realistas y se dividen en capítulos. Las soluciones comienzan en la página (💡⇨) 74. Un pequeño círculo en la parte inferior derecha de cada diagrama indica qué color está jugando y es su turno. La notación de las soluciones corresponde aproximadamente a la notación algebraica abreviada internacional. Las jugadas se numeran a partir de la situación mostrada, además se ha Introducido un asterisco (*), que marca cualquier jugada legal. Ocasionalmente también se dieron soluciones alternativas. No se garantiza la integridad y corrección de las soluciones.

FEN como códigos QR

Las notaciones de Forsyth-Edwards (FEN) de todos los rompecabezas se proporcionan como códigos QR al final de este libro. Esto le permite cargar la posición inicial de cada rompecabezas en cualquier aplicación de ajedrez compatible con FEN simplemente escaneando el código dado. Las soluciones no están incluidas en los códigos QR.

Consejos de uso

Por supuesto, depende de ti cómo resuelves los acertijos de este libro. No obstante, me gustaría ofrecerle algunas sugerencias que pueden mejorar la "experiencia del usuario".

- **No vayas en orden**
  Si mira regularmente las soluciones (para verificar una solución encontrada o para buscar una solución de un rompecabezas sin resolver), entonces no revise los rompecabezas en orden. Miras demasiado rápido las soluciones vecinas y accidentalmente podrías llevarte el primer movimiento o incluso la solución completa del siguiente rompecabezas contigo.

- **Resuelve los acertijos en un tablero real**
  Esto es, por supuesto, una cuestión de gusto, pero personal-mente me parece más agradable configurar la situación del juego en un tablero real, especialmente porque resolver una posición en un tablero también entrena enormemente la percepción espacial de las piezas y sus ángulos de ataque.

- **Juega en ambas partes**
  Especialmente con los problemas "más largos", un jaque mate a menudo es posible en menos movimientos si los contra-movimientos no son forzados y el lado contrario reacciona imprudentemente. Siempre trate de encontrar el mejor movimiento posible para que el oponente extienda el juego.

Eröffnung

Über dieses Buch

Auf den folgenden Seiten finden Sie mehr als 200 Schachprobleme, die in nur wenigen Zügen mit Schachmatt enden. Die Rätsel basieren auf realistischen Spielsituationen und sind unterteilt in Kapitel. Die Lösungen finden Sie ab Seite (🔆⇨) 74. Ein kleiner Kreis unten rechts in jedem Diagramm gibt an, welche Farbe Sie spielen und Sie sind am Zug. Die Notation der Lösungen entspricht in ungefähr der internationalen figürlichen algebraischen Kurznotation. Die Züge sind ab der abgebildeten Situation nummeriert, zusätzlich wurde ein Asterisk (*) eingeführt, welcher einen beliebigen legalen Zug kennzeichnet. Alternative Lösungen werden gelegentlich auch angegeben. Eine Vollständigkeit und Richtigkeit der Lösungen ist nicht gewährleistet.

Forsyth-Edwards-Notation als QR-Codes

Forsyth-Edwards-Notationen (FEN) aller Rätsel sind als QR-Codes am Ende dieses Buchs angegeben. Auf diese Weise können Sie die Startposition jedes Rätsels in jede Schach-App laden, die das FEN unterstützt, indem Sie einfach den angegebenen Code scannen. Die Lösungen sind nicht in den QR-Codes enthalten.

Tipps zur Benutzung

Es ist Ihnen natürlich selbst überlassen, wie Sie die Rätsel in diesem Buch lösen. Nichtsdestotrotz möchte ich Ihnen ein paar Vorschläge unterbreiten, die das „Anwendererlebnis" eventuell verbessern.

- **Gehen Sie nicht der Reihe nach**
  Wenn Sie regelmäßig in die Lösungen schauen (um eine gefundene Lösung zu verifizieren oder ein nicht gelöstes Rätsel aufzulösen), dann gehen Sie die Rätsel nicht der Reihe nach durch. Zu schnell guckt man auf die benachbarten Lösungen und nimmt versehentlich den ersten Zug oder gar den ganzen Lösungsweg des nächsten Rätsels mit.

- **Lösen Sie die Rätsel am Brett**
  Es ist natürlich Geschmackssache, aber ich persönlich finde es angenehmer, die Spielsituation auf einem echten Brett aufzubauen, zumal das Lösen einer Stellung auf einem Brett auch die räumliche Wahrnehmung von Figuren und deren Angriffswinkel enorm schult.

- **Spielen Sie beide Seiten**
  Gerade bei den „längeren" Problemen ist oft bei nicht erzwungenen Zügen und unklugen Reaktionen der Gegenseite ein Schachmatt in weniger Zügen möglich. Versuchen Sie immer, den bestmöglichen Zug für den Gegner zu finden, um das Spiel zu verlängern.

Otwarcie

O tej książce

Na kolejnych stronach znajdziesz ponad 200 zadań szachowych, które w kilku ruchach zakończą się matem. Zagadki oparte są na realistycznych sytuacjach w grze i podzielone są na rozdziały. Rozwiązania zaczynają się na stronie (🔍⇨) 74. Małe kółko w prawym dolnym rogu każdego diagramu wskazuje, jaki kolor grasz i jest twoja kolej. Zapis rozwiązań odpowiada w przybliżeniu międzynarodowej skróconej notacji algebraicznej. Ruchy są ponumerowane od pokazanej sytuacji, dodatkowo wprowadzono gwiazdkę (*), która oznacza każdy legalny ruch. Od czasu do czasu podawano również alternatywne rozwiązania. Nie gwarantuje się kompletności i poprawności rozwiązań.

Notacja Forsytha-Edwardsa jako kody QR

Notacje Forsytha-Edwardsa (FEN) wszystkich łamigłówek są podane jako kody QR na końcu tej książki. Dzięki temu możesz załadować początkową pozycję każdej łamigłówki do dowolnej aplikacji szachowej, która obsługuje FEN, po prostu skanując podany kod. Rozwiązania nie są zawarte w kodach QR.

Wskazówki dotyczące użytkowania

Oczywiście od Ciebie zależy, jak rozwiążesz zagadki zawarte w tej książce. Niemniej jednak chciałbym przedstawić kilka sugestii, które mogą poprawić „doświadczenie użytkownika".

- **Nie idź w porządku**
  Jeśli regularnie przeglądasz rozwiązania (by zweryfikować znalezione rozwiązanie lub wyszukać rozwiązanie nierozwiązanej łamigłówki), nie przeglądaj łamigłówek po kolei. Zbyt szybko patrzysz na sąsiednie rozwiązania i przypadkowo możesz zabrać ze sobą pierwszy ruch lub nawet całe rozwiązanie kolejnej zagadki.

- **Rozwiązuj zagadki na prawdziwej planszy**
  To oczywiście kwestia gustu, ale osobiście uważam, że przyjemniej jest ustawić sytuację w grze na prawdziwej planszy, zwłaszcza że rozwiązywanie pozycji na planszy ogromnie trenuje również przestrzenną percepcję pionów i ich kąty ataku.

- **Zagraj w obie strony**
  Zwłaszcza w przypadku „dłuższych" problemów często możliwy jest mat w mniejszej liczbie ruchów, jeśli kontrruchy nie są wymuszone, a przeciwna strona reaguje nierozsądnie. Zawsze staraj się znaleźć najlepszy możliwy ruch dla przeciwnika, aby przedłużyć grę.

Opening

Over dit boek

Op de volgende pagina's vindt u meer dan 200 schaakproblemen die in slechts enkele zetten schaakmat eindigen. De puzzels zijn gebaseerd op realistische spelsituaties en zijn onderverdeeld in hoofdstukken. De oplossingen beginnen op pagina (🔅⇨) 74. Een kleine cirkel rechtsonder in elk diagram geeft aan welke kleur je speelt en jij bent aan de beurt. De notatie van de oplossingen komt ongeveer overeen met de internationale steno-algebraïsche notatie. De zetten zijn genummerd vanaf de getoonde situatie, daarnaast is er een asterisk (*) toegevoegd, die elke legale zet markeert. Af en toe werden ook alternatieve oplossingen gegeven. Een volledigheid en correctheid van de oplossingen wordt niet gegarandeerd.

Forsyth-Edwards-notatie als QR-codes

Aan het einde van elk hoofdstuk vind je alle puzzels terug in Forsyth Edwards Notation (FEN) als QR-codes. Hiermee kun je de startpositie van elke puzzel in elke schaak-app laden die de FEN ondersteunt, simpelweg door de gegeven code te scannen. De oplossingen zijn niet opgenomen in de QR-codes.

Tips voor gebruik

Het is natuurlijk aan jou hoe je de puzzels in dit boek oplost. Toch wil ik u enkele suggesties meegeven die de "gebruikerservaring" kunnen verbeteren.

- **Ga niet in volgorde**
  Als je regelmatig naar de oplossingen kijkt (om een gevonden oplossing te verifiëren of om een oplossing van een onopgeloste puzzel op te zoeken), ga dan niet op volgorde door de puzzels. Je kijkt te snel naar de aangrenzende oplossingen en neemt per ongeluk de eerste zet of zelfs de hele oplossing van de volgende puzzel mee.

- **Los de puzzels op een echt bord op**
  Dit is natuurlijk een kwestie van smaak, maar persoonlijk vind ik het prettiger om de spelsituatie op een echt bord op te zetten, vooral omdat het oplossen van een stelling op een bord ook de ruimtelijke waarneming van stukken en hun aanvalshoeken enorm traint.

- **Speel beide partijen**
  Vooral bij de "langere" opgaven is schaakmat vaak mogelijk in minder zetten als tegenzetten niet geforceerd worden en de tegenpartij onverstandig reageert. Probeer altijd de best mogelijke zet voor de tegenstander te vinden om het spel te verlengen.

Malfermo

Pri ĉi tiu libro

En la sekvaj paĝoj vi trovos pli ol 200 ŝakproblemojn, kiuj finiĝos per mato en nur kelkaj movoj. La enigmoj baziĝas sur realismaj ludsituacioj kaj estas divivitaj en ĉapitrojn. La solvoj komenciĝas sur paĝo () 74. Malgranda rondo malsupre dekstre de ĉiu diagramo indikas kiun koloron vi ludas kaj estas via vico. La notacio de la solvoj respondas proksimume al la internacia stenografia algebra notacio. La movoj estas numeritaj de la montrita situacio, krome asterisko (*) estis enkondukita, kiu markas ajnan leĝan movon. Alternativaj solvoj ankaŭ estis foje donitaj. Pleneco kaj ĝusteco de la solvoj ne estas garantiitaj.

Forsyth-Edwards-notacio kiel QR-kodoj

Forsyth-Edwards Notacioj (FEN) de ĉiuj enigmoj estas provizitaj kiel QR-kodoj ĉe la fino de ĉi tiu libro. Ĉi tio ebligas al vi ŝargi la komencan pozicion de ĉiu enigmo en ajnan ŝakprogramon kiu subtenas la FEN simple skanante la donitan kodon. La solvoj ne estas inkluzivitaj en la QR-kodoj.

eo

Konsiloj por uzo

Kompreneble dependas de vi kiel vi solvas la enigmojn en ĉi tiu libro. Tamen mi ŝatus proponi al vi kelkajn sugestojn, kiuj eble plibonigos la "uzantsperton".

- **Ne procedu lineare**

  Se vi regule rigardas la solvojn (por kontroli trovitan solvon aŭ por solvi nesolvitan enigmon), tiam vi ne trapasas la enigmojn en ordo. Vi tro rapide rigardas la najbarajn solvojn kaj hazarde kunportas la unuan movon aŭ eĉ la tutan solvon de la sekva enigmo.

- **Solvu la enigmojn sur la tabulo**

  Kompreneble temas pri gusto, sed persone mi trovas pli agrable starigi la ludsituacion sur reala tabulo, precipe ĉar solvi pozicion sur tabulo tre trejnas ankaŭ la spacan percepton de pecoj kaj ties atakanguloj.

- **Ludu ambaŭ flankojn**

  Precipe kun la "pli longaj" problemoj, mato ofte eblas en malpli da movoj se la movoj ne estas devigitaj kaj la alia flanko reagas malprudente. Ĉiam provu trovi la plej bonan eblan movon por la kontraŭulo por etendi la ludon.

in 2

mate in two
mat en deux
mate en dos
matt in zwei
mat w dwóch
mat in twee
mato en du

in 2

Nº 1

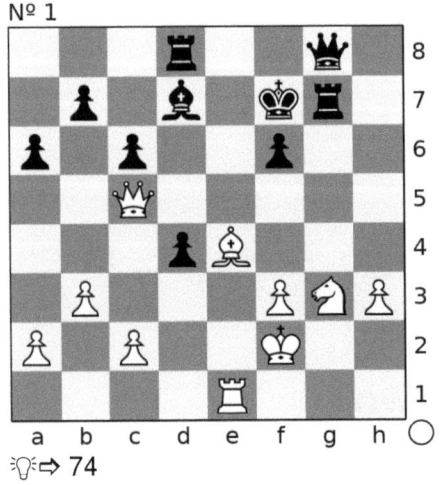

🔅⇨ 74

Nº 2

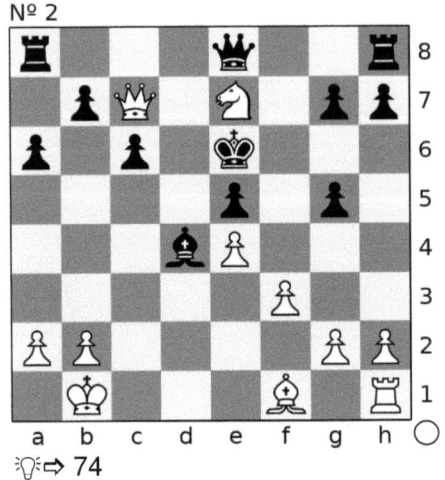

🔅⇨ 74

Nº 3

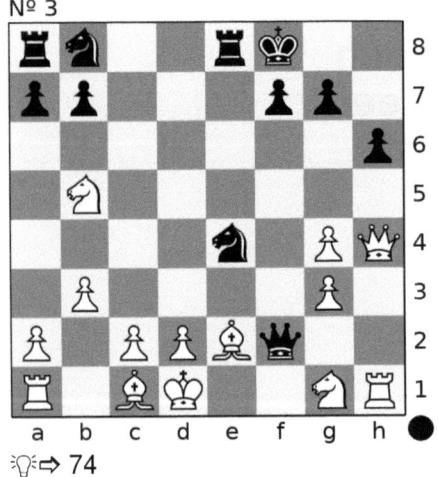

🔅⇨ 74

Nº 4

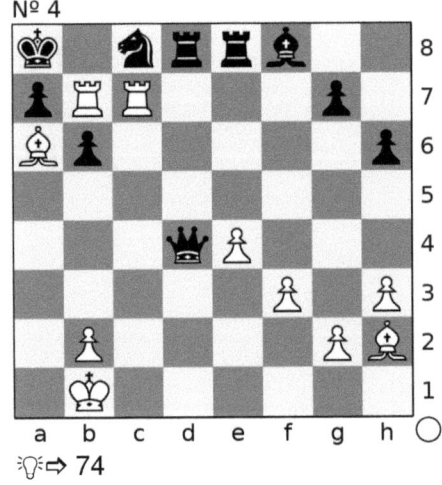

🔅⇨ 74

in 2

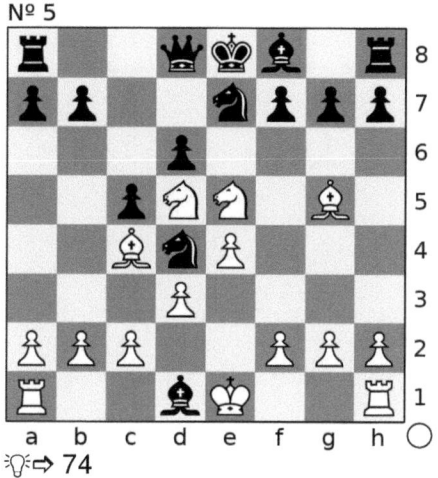

№ 5

a b c d e f g h ○

🔅⇨ 74

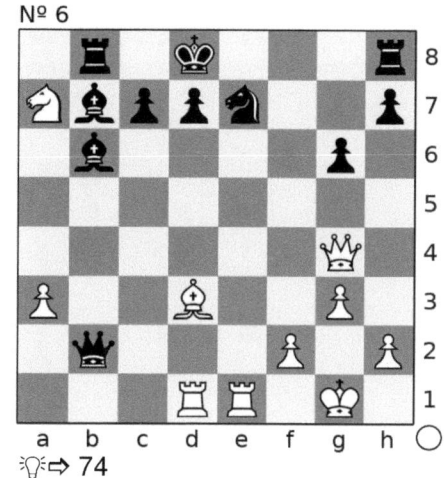

№ 6

a b c d e f g h ○

🔅⇨ 74

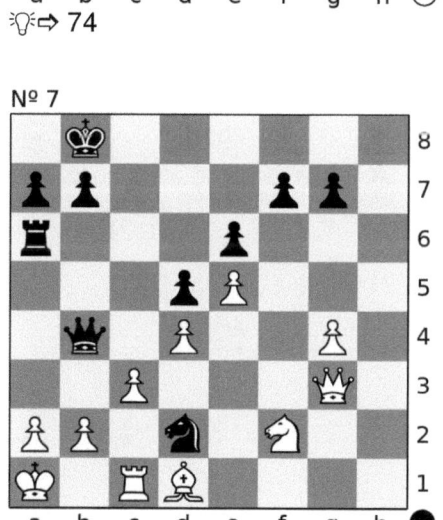

№ 7

a b c d e f g h ●

🔅⇨ 74

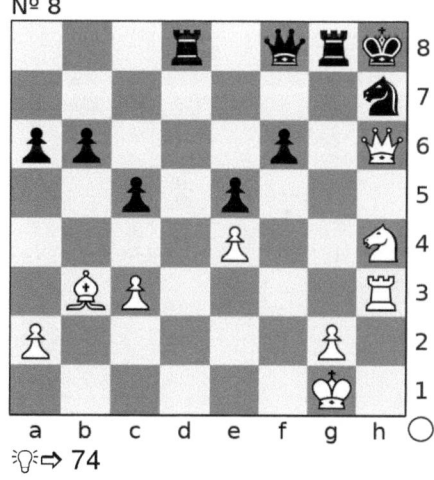

№ 8

a b c d e f g h ○

🔅⇨ 74

in 2

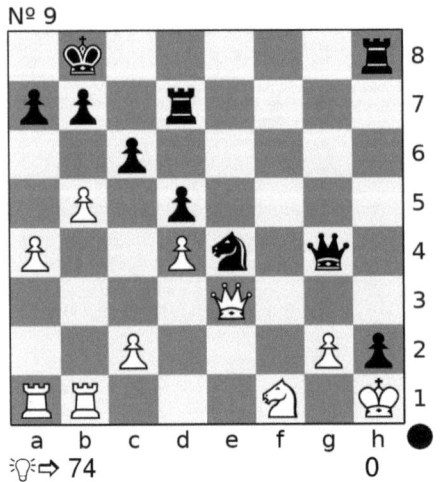

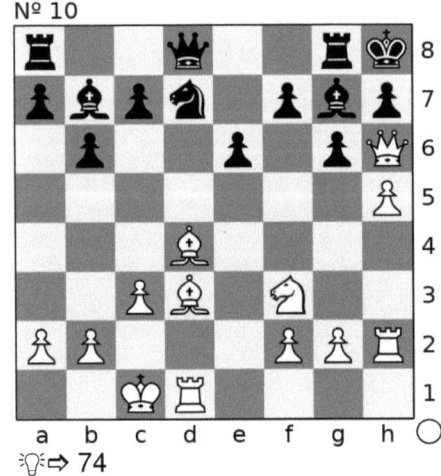

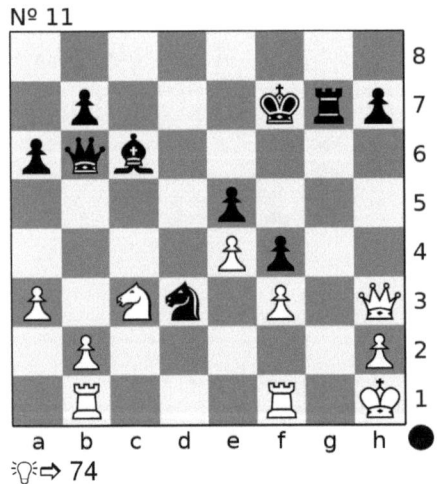

in 2

№ 13

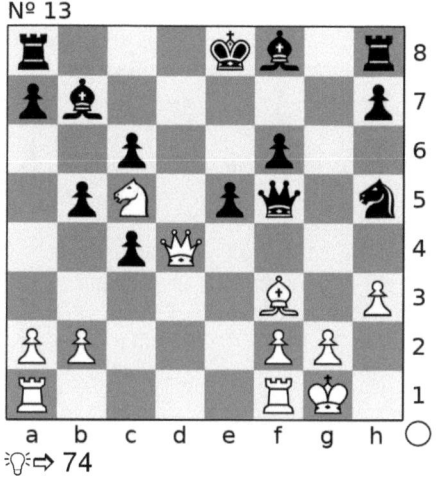

💡⇨ 74

№ 14

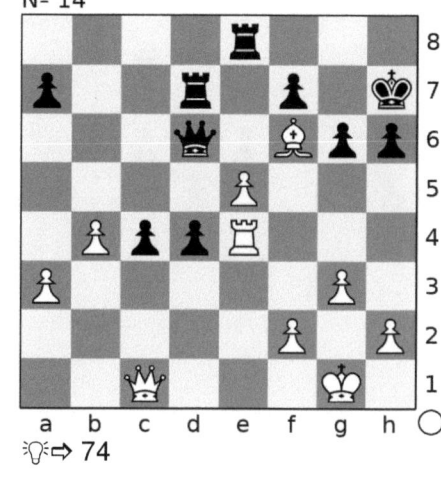

💡⇨ 74

№ 15

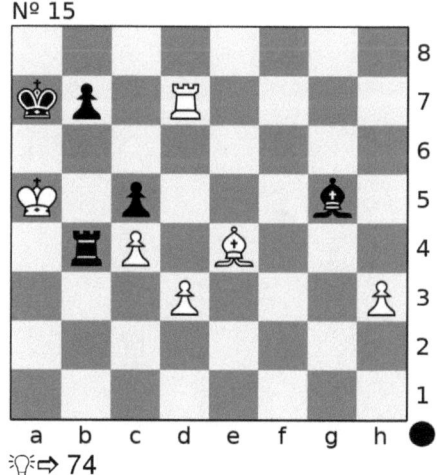

💡⇨ 74

№ 16

💡⇨ 74

in 2

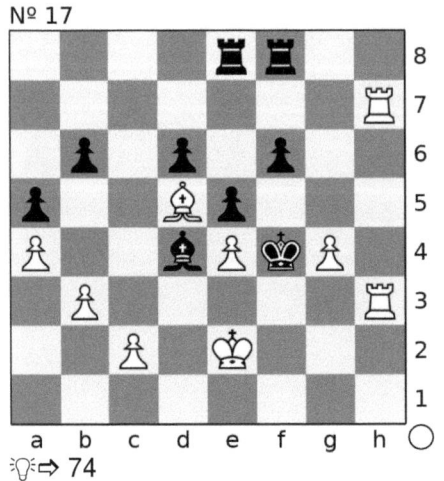

a b c d e f g h ○
💡⇨ 74

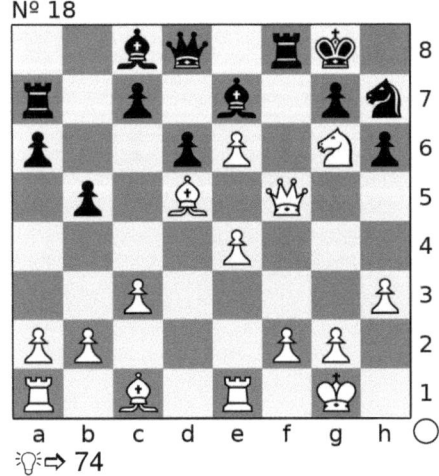

a b c d e f g h ○
💡⇨ 74

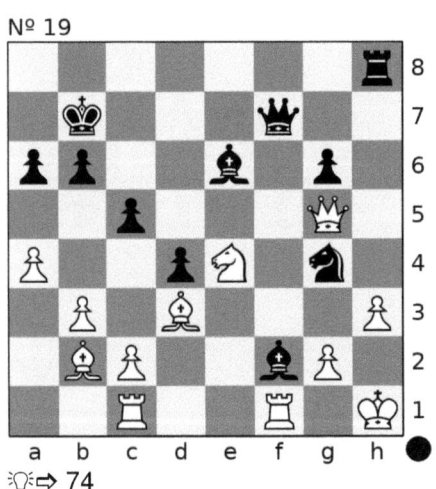

a b c d e f g h ●
💡⇨ 74

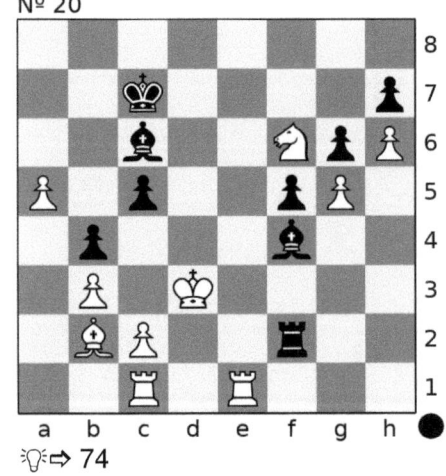

a b c d e f g h ●
💡⇨ 74

№ 21

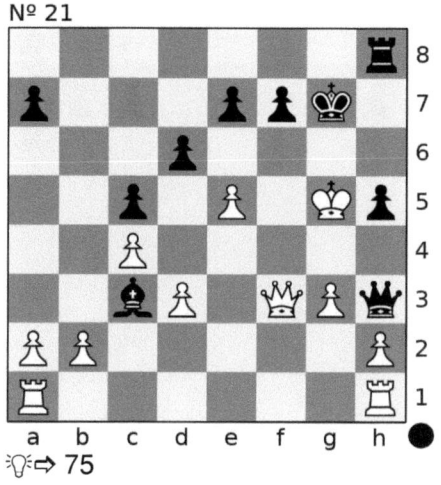

a b c d e f g h ●
🔅⇨ 75

№ 22

a b c d e f g h ●
🔅⇨ 75

№ 23

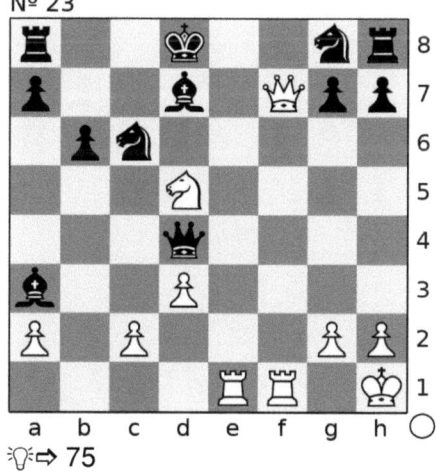

a b c d e f g h ○
🔅⇨ 75

№ 24

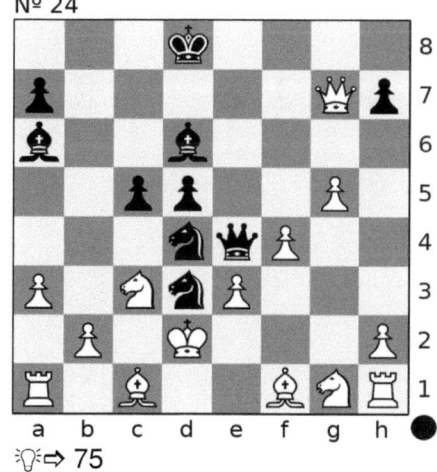

a b c d e f g h ●
🔅⇨ 75

in 2

№ 25

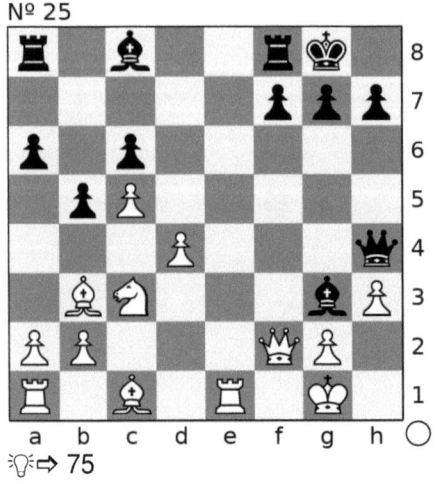

a b c d e f g h ○
💡⇨ 75

№ 26

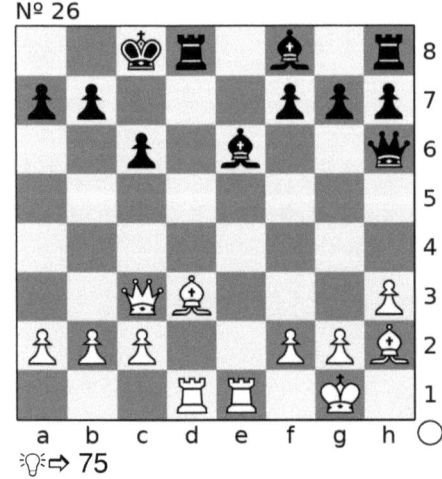

a b c d e f g h ○
💡⇨ 75

№ 27

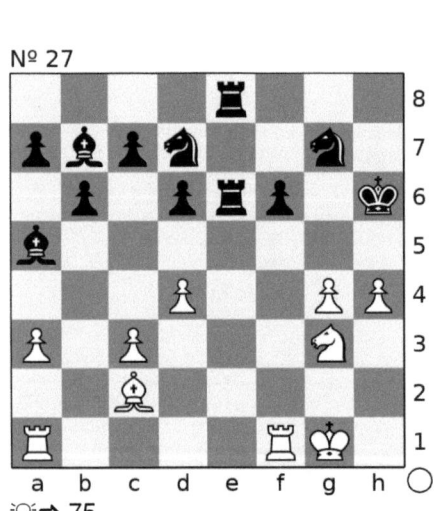

a b c d e f g h ○
💡⇨ 75

№ 28

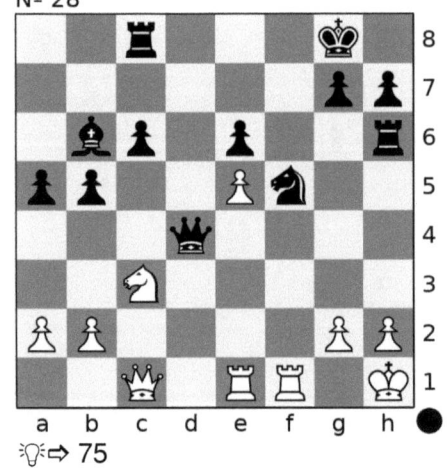

a b c d e f g h ●
💡⇨ 75

in 2

№ 29

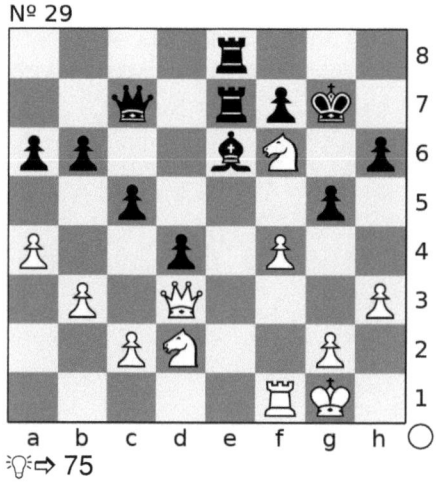

a b c d e f g h ○
💡⇨ 75

№ 30

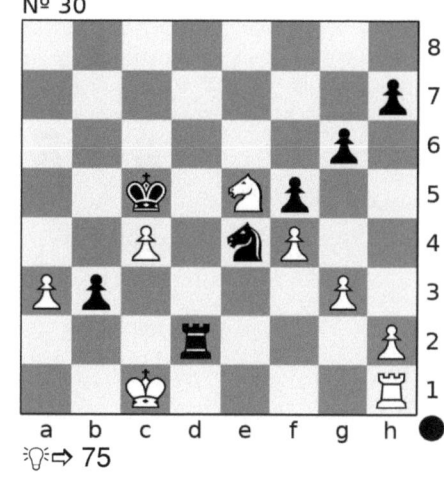

a b c d e f g h ●
💡⇨ 75

№ 31

a b c d e f g h ○
💡⇨ 75

№ 32

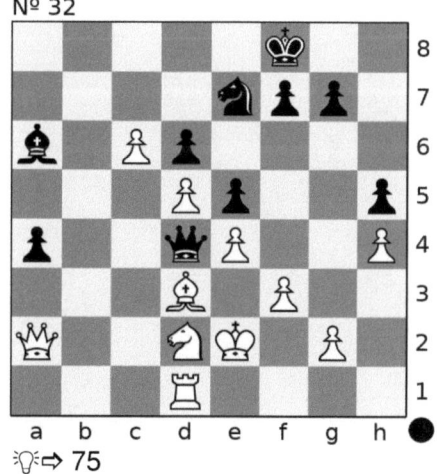

a b c d e f g h ●
💡⇨ 75

in 2

Nº 33

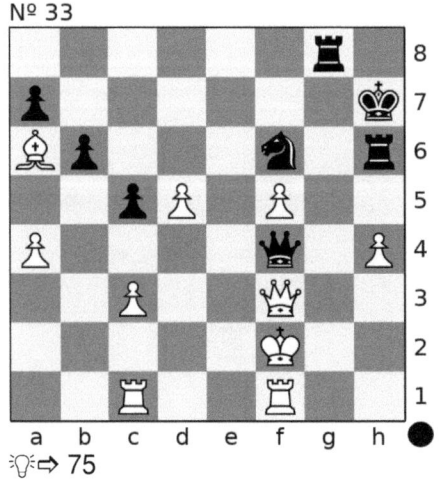

🔆⇨ 75

Nº 34

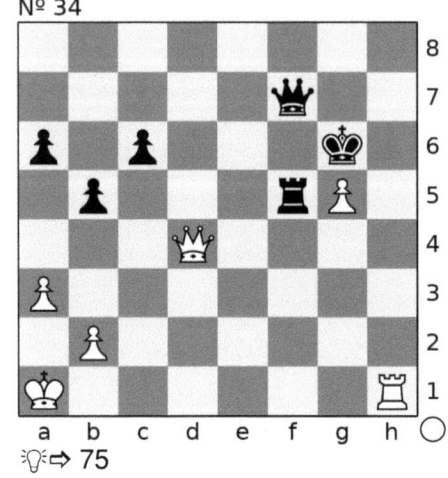

🔆⇨ 75

Nº 35

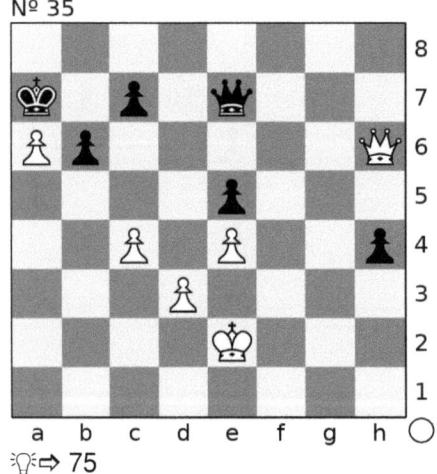

🔆⇨ 75

Nº 36

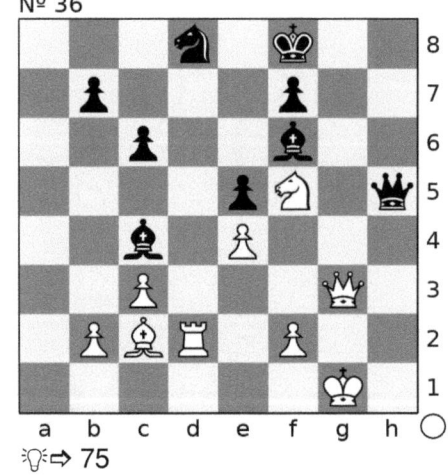

🔆⇨ 75

in 2

№ 37

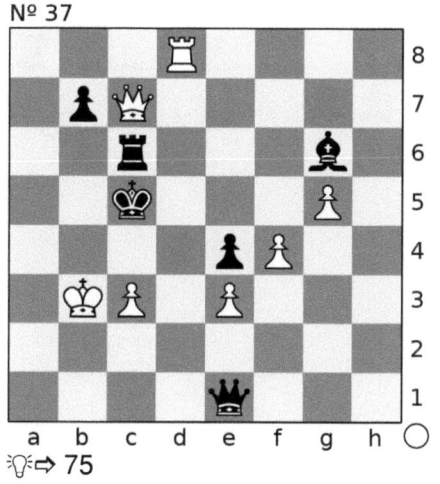

a b c d e f g h ○
💡⇨ 75

№ 38

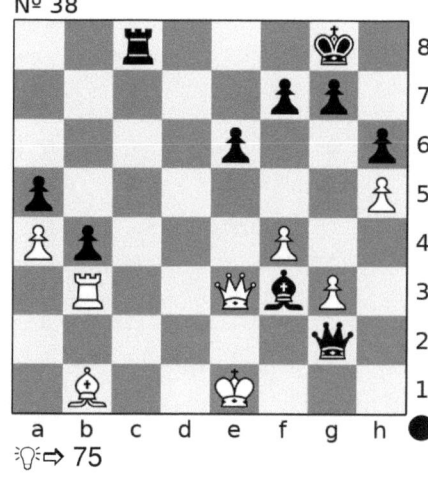

a b c d e f g h ●
💡⇨ 75

№ 39

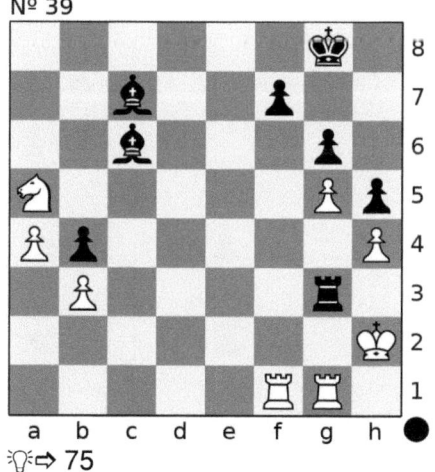

a b c d e f g h ●
💡⇨ 75

№ 40

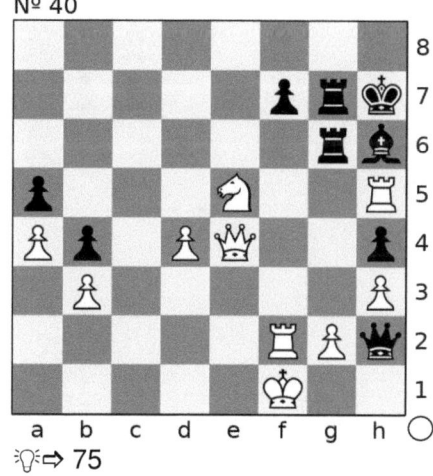

a b c d e f g h ○
💡⇨ 75

in 2

№ 41

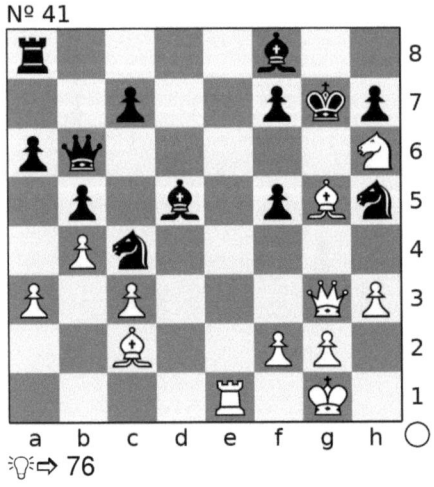

a b c d e f g h ○
💡⇨ 76

№ 42

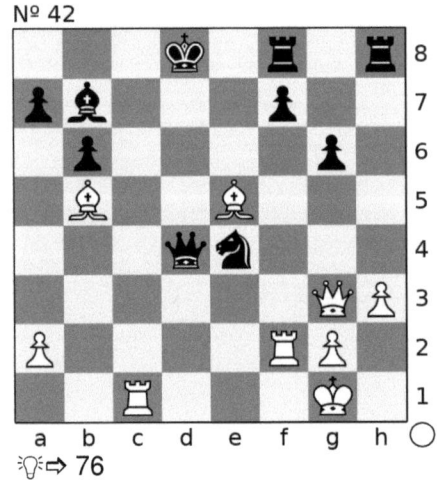

a b c d e f g h ○
💡⇨ 76

№ 43

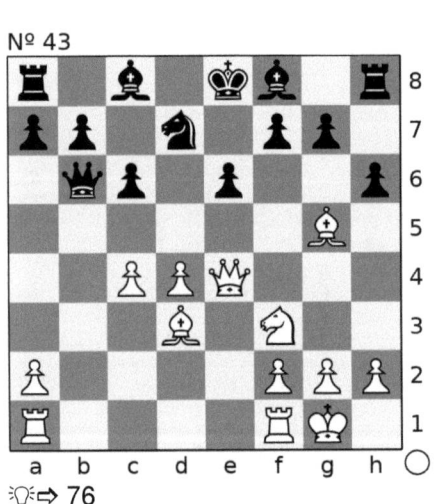

a b c d e f g h ○
💡⇨ 76

№ 44

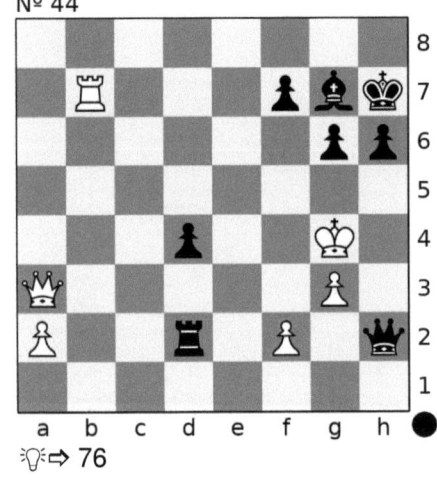

a b c d e f g h ●
💡⇨ 76

in 2

№ 45

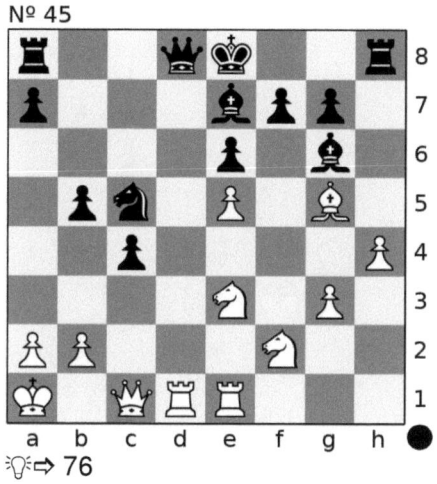

🔆⇨ 76

№ 46

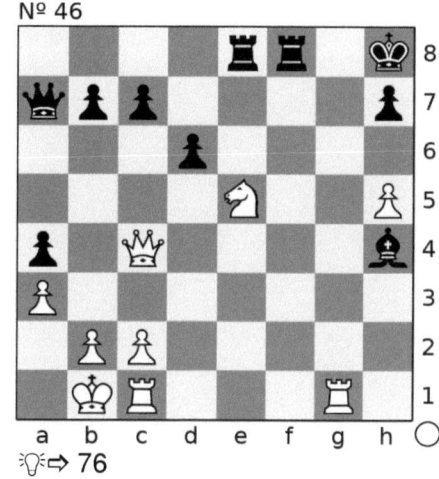

🔆⇨ 76

№ 47

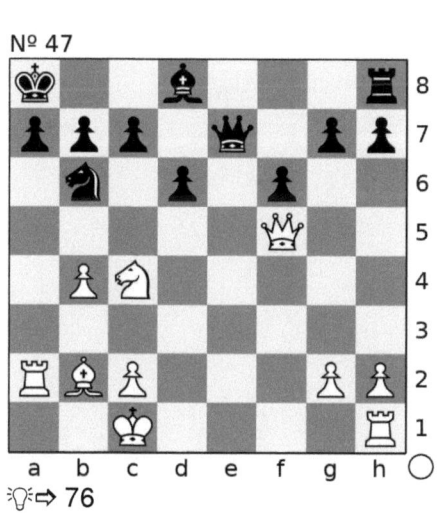

🔆⇨ 76

№ 48

🔆⇨ 76

29

in 2

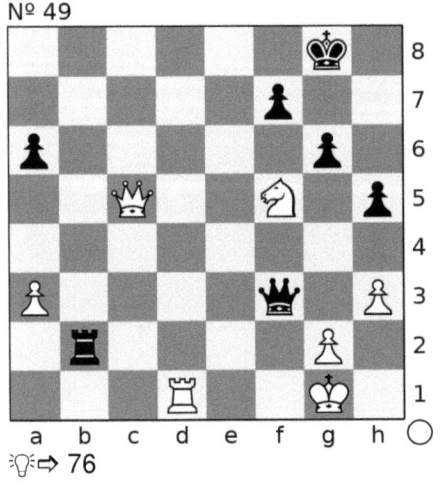

8 7 6 5 4 3 2 1
a b c d e f g h ○

🔅⇨ 76

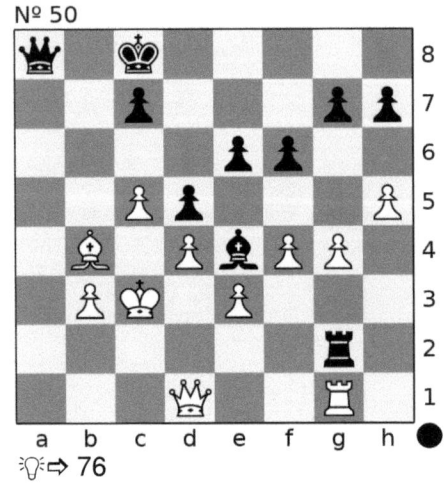

8 7 6 5 4 3 2 1
a b c d e f g h ●

🔅⇨ 76

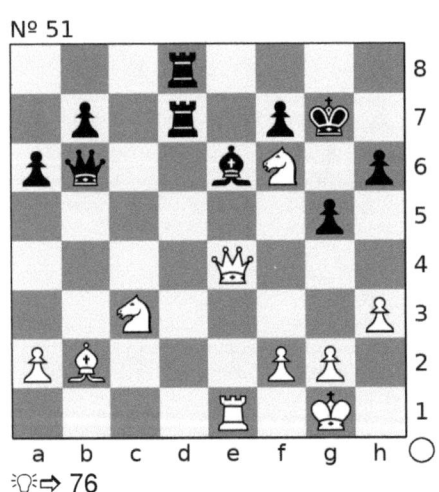

8 7 6 5 4 3 2 1
a b c d e f g h ○

🔅⇨ 76

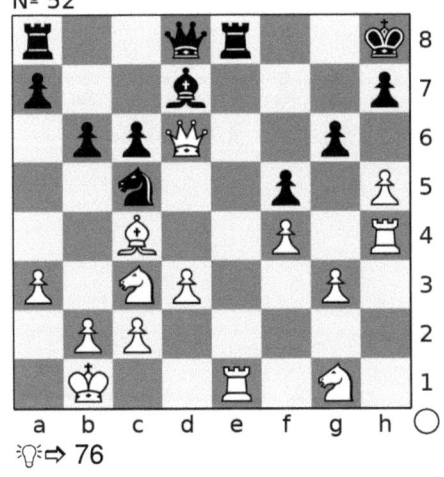

8 7 6 5 4 3 2 1
a b c d e f g h ○

🔅⇨ 76

in 2

№ 53

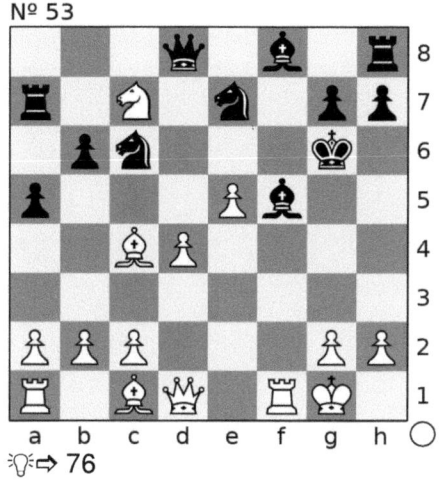

☀⇨ 76

№ 54

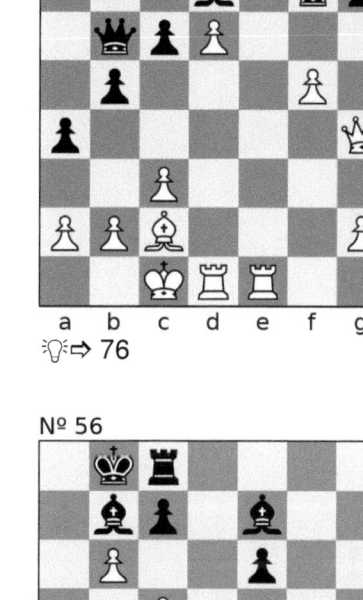

☀⇨ 76

№ 55

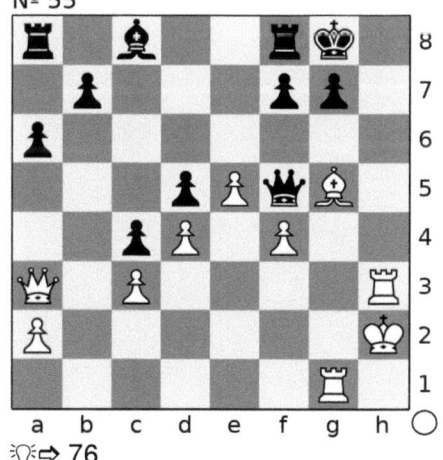

☀⇨ 76

№ 56

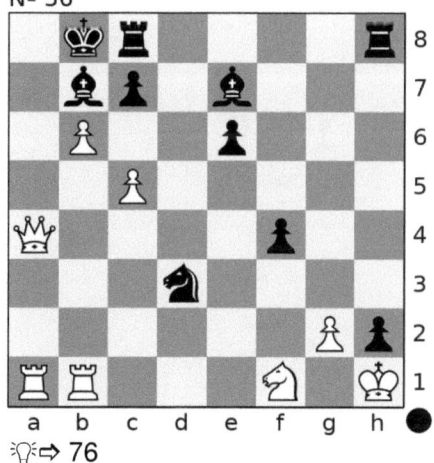

☀⇨ 76

in 2

№ 57

№ 58

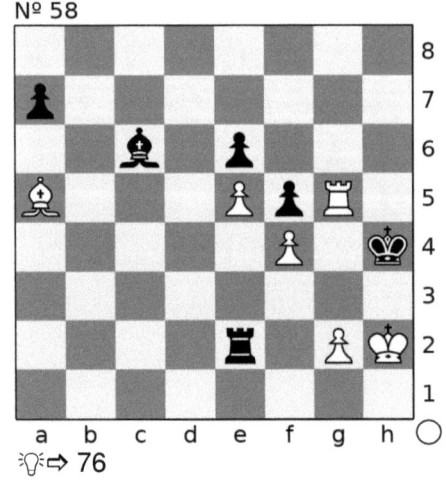

№ 59

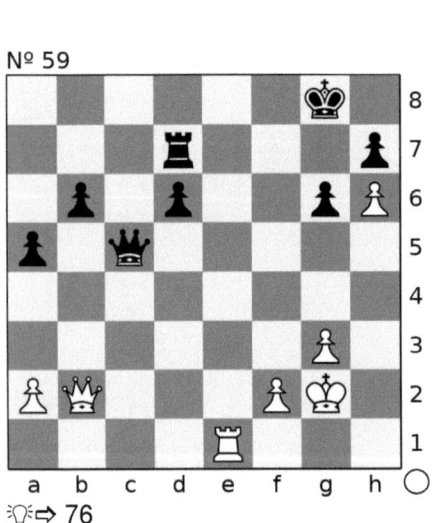

№ 60

 # in 3

mate in three
mat en trois
mate en tres
matt in drei
mat w trzech
mat in drie
mato en tri

in 3

№ 61

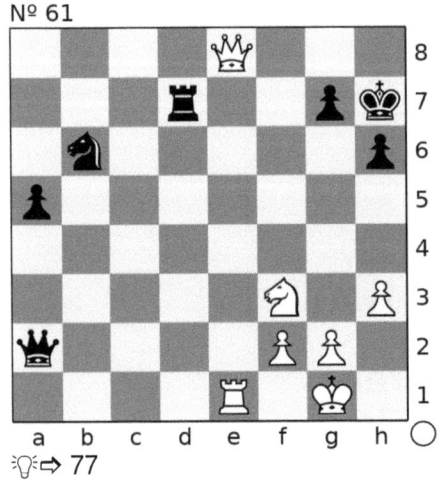

a b c d e f g h ○
💡⇨ 77

№ 62

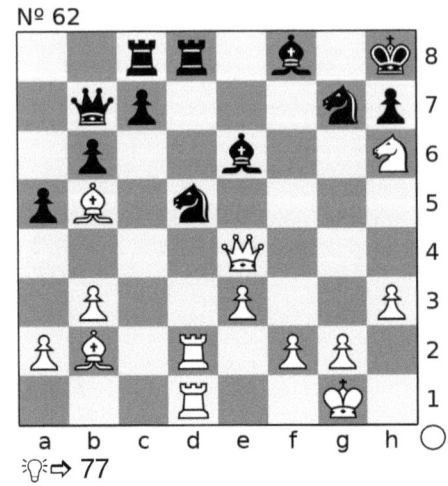

a b c d e f g h ○
💡⇨ 77

№ 63

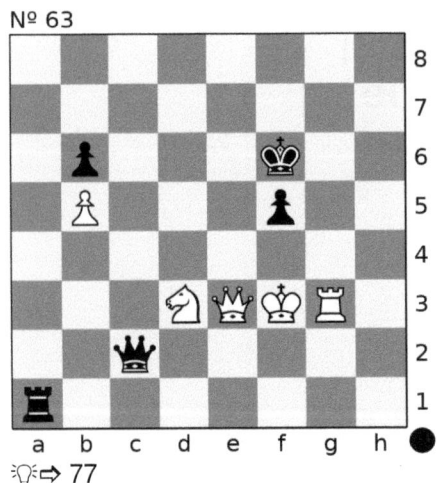

a b c d e f g h ●
💡⇨ 77

№ 64

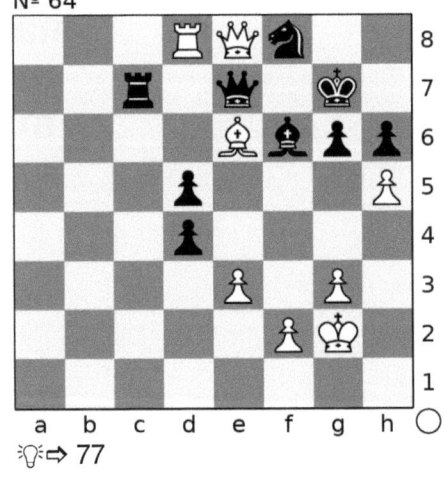

a b c d e f g h ○
💡⇨ 77

№ 65

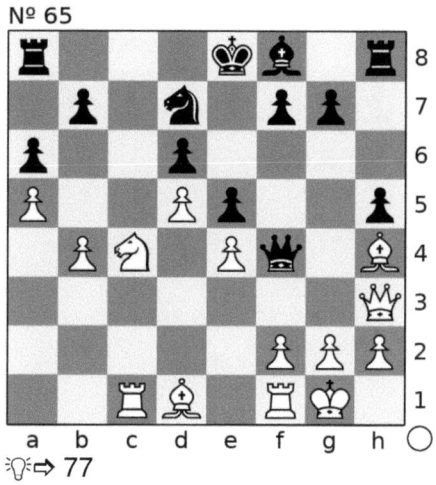

a b c d e f g h ○
💡⇨ 77

№ 66

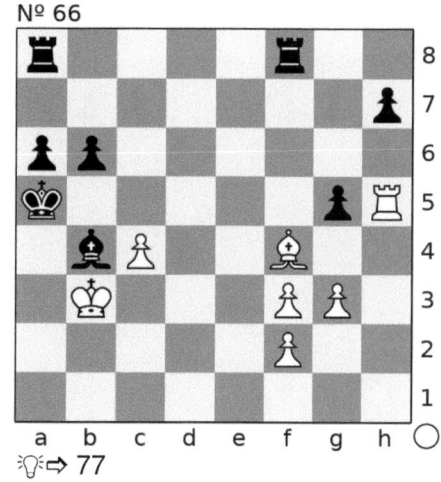

a b c d e f g h ○
💡⇨ 77

№ 67

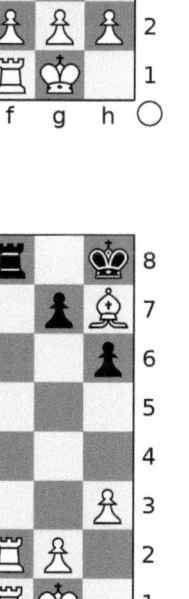

a b c d e f g h ○
💡⇨ 77

№ 68

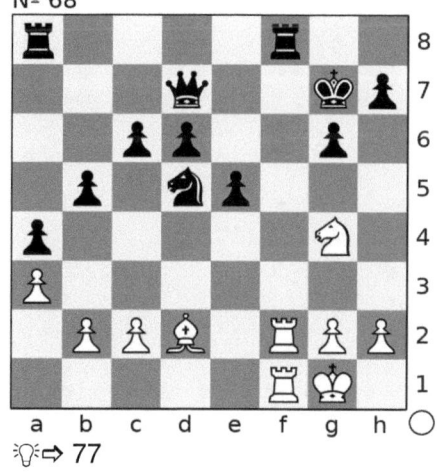

a b c d e f g h ○
💡⇨ 77

in 3

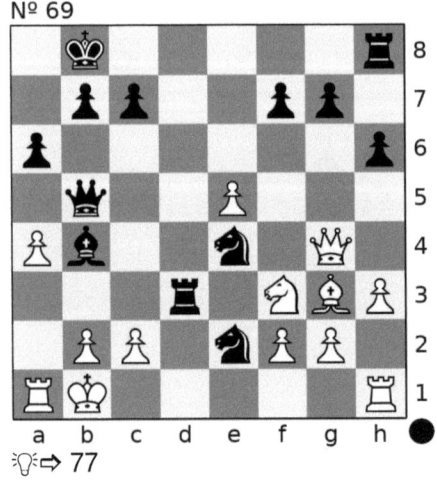

№ 69

🔦⇨ 77

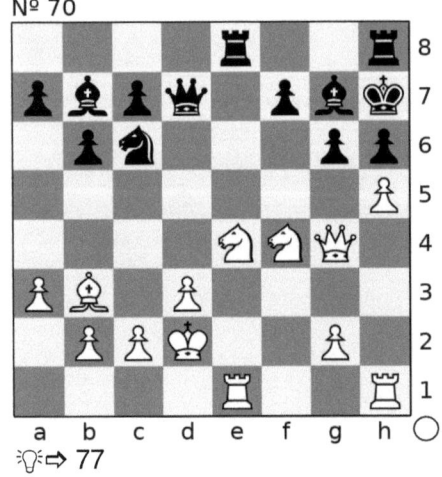

№ 70

🔦⇨ 77

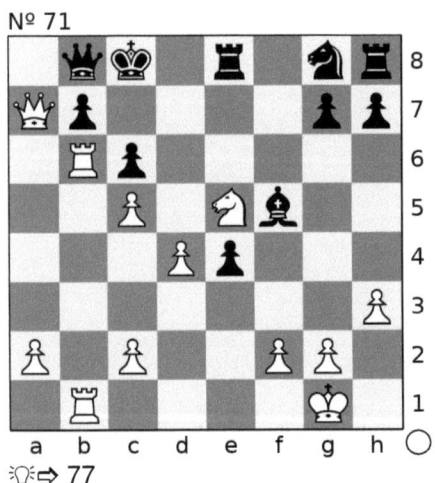

№ 71

🔦⇨ 77

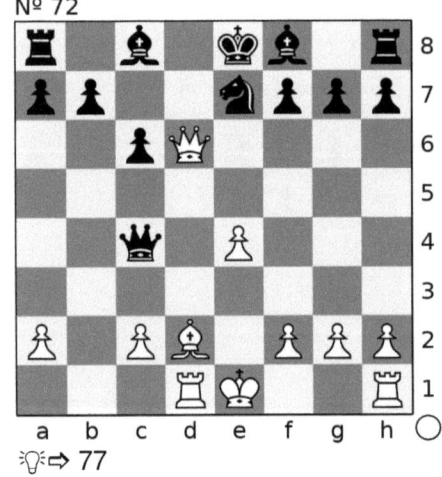

№ 72

🔦⇨ 77

in 3

№ 73

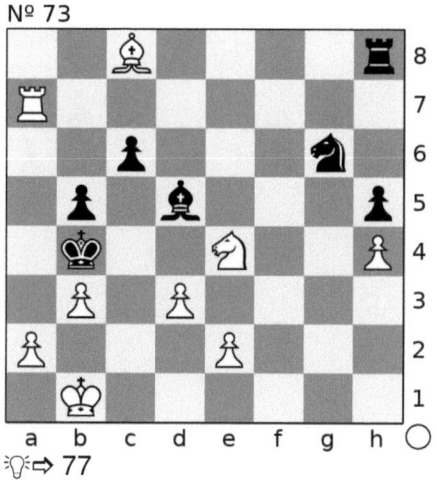

💡⇨ 77

№ 74

💡⇨ 77

№ 75

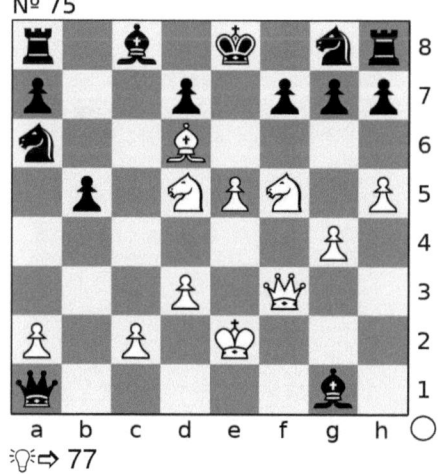

💡⇨ 77

№ 76

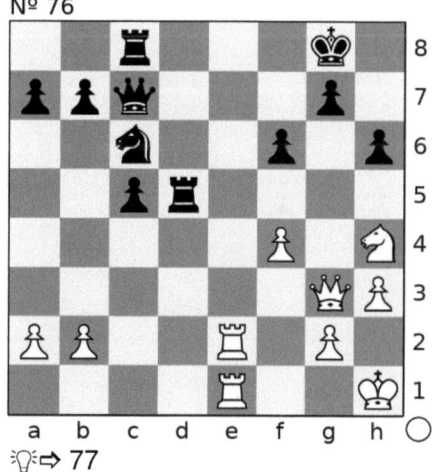

💡⇨ 77

in 3

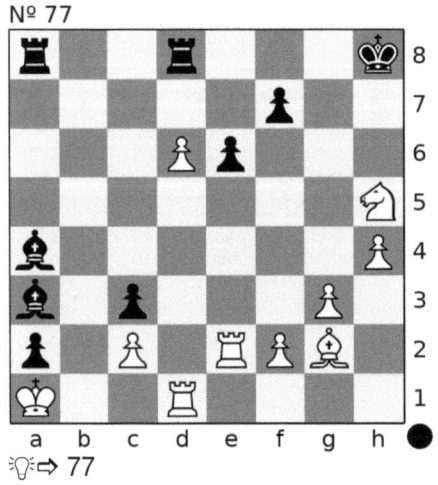

№ 78

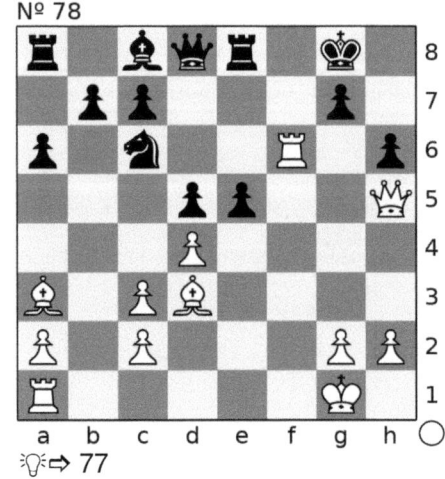

№ 79

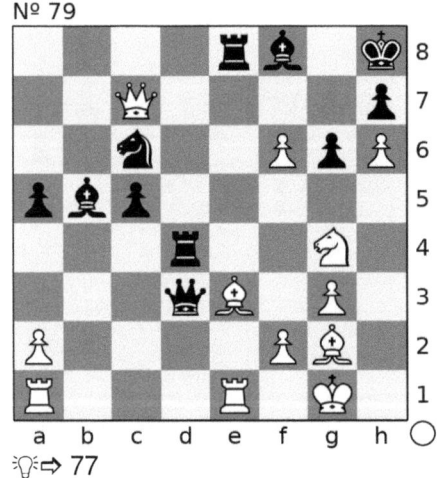

№ 80

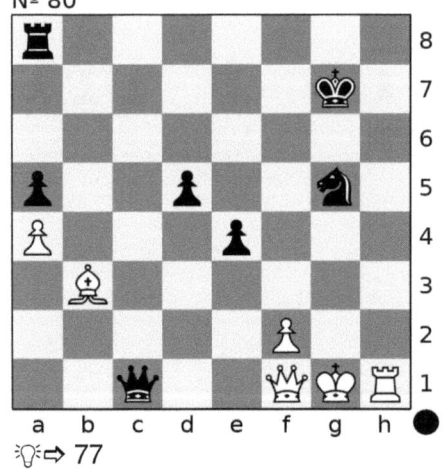

💡⇨ 77

38

in 3

№ 81

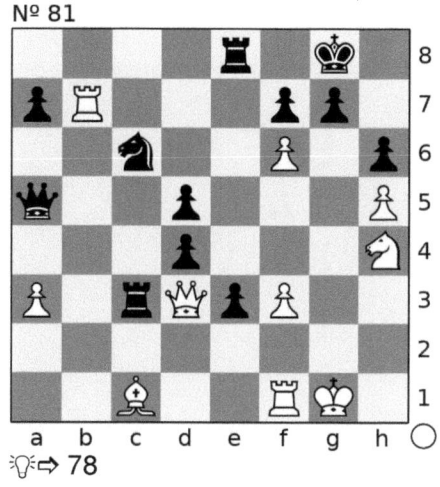

💡⇨ 78

№ 82

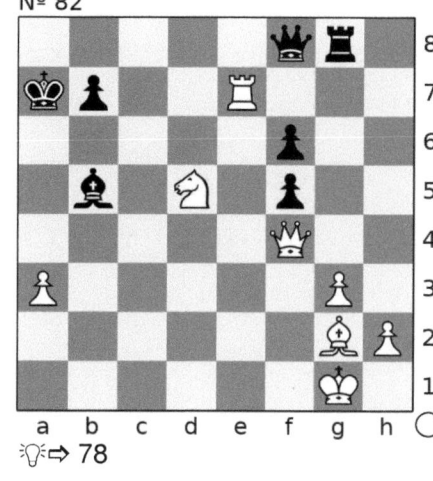

💡⇨ 78

№ 83

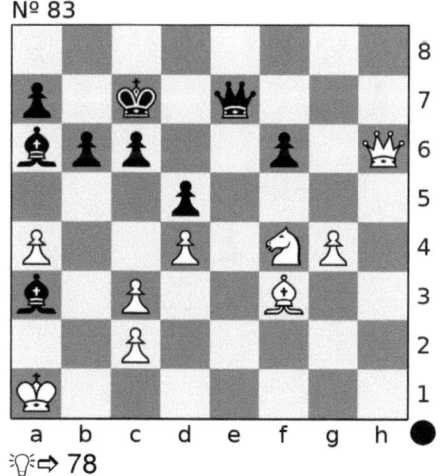

💡⇨ 78

№ 84

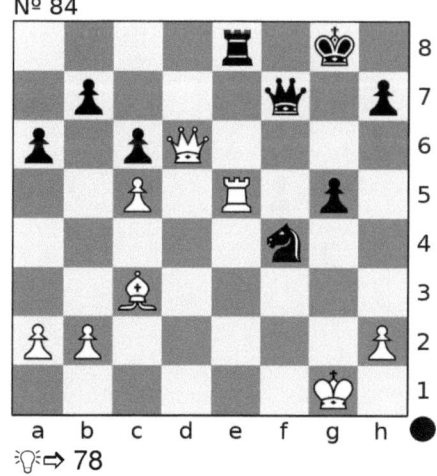

💡⇨ 78

in 3

№ 85

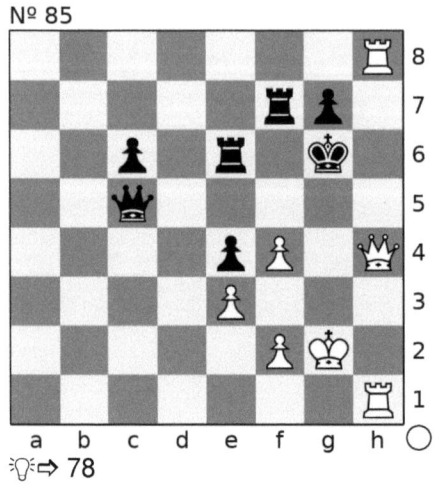

a b c d e f g h

○

🔅⇨ 78

№ 86

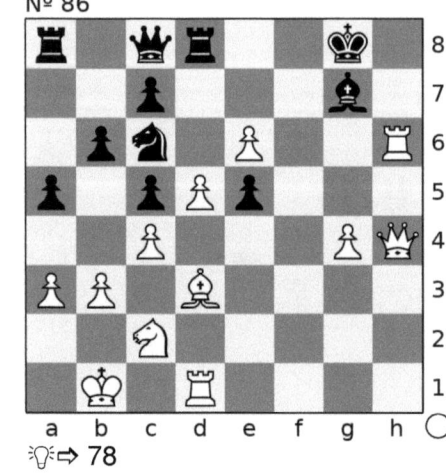

a b c d e f g h

○

🔅⇨ 78

№ 87

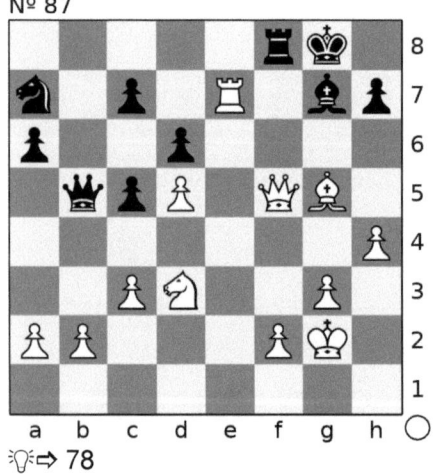

a b c d e f g h

○

🔅⇨ 78

№ 88

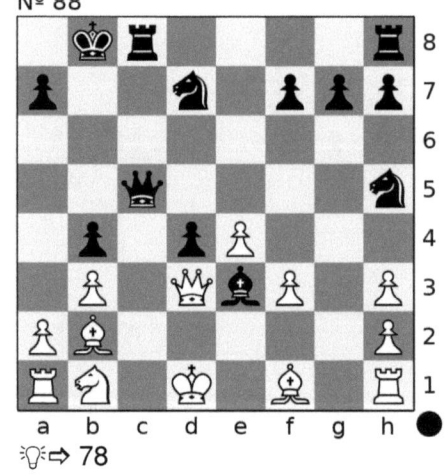

a b c d e f g h

●

🔅⇨ 78

№ 89

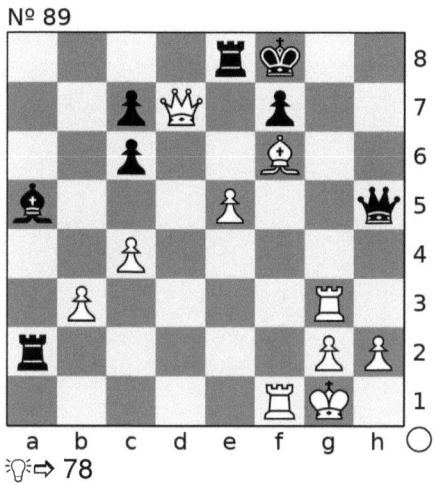

💡⇨ 78

№ 90

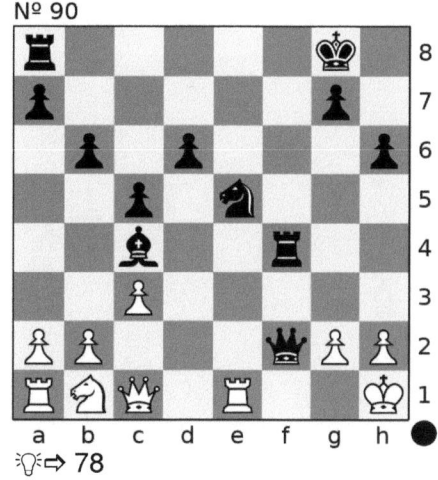

💡⇨ 78

№ 91

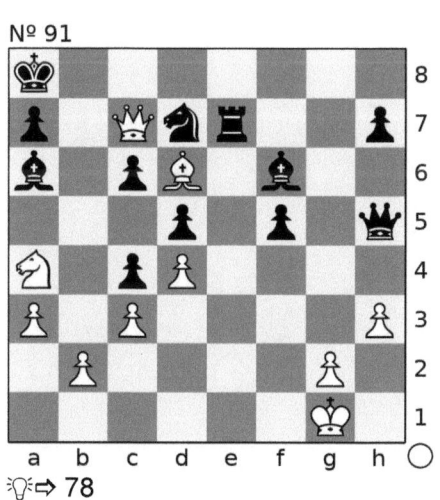

💡⇨ 78

№ 92

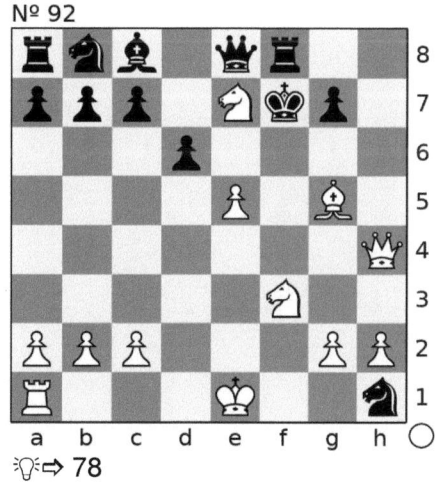

💡⇨ 78

in 3

№ 93

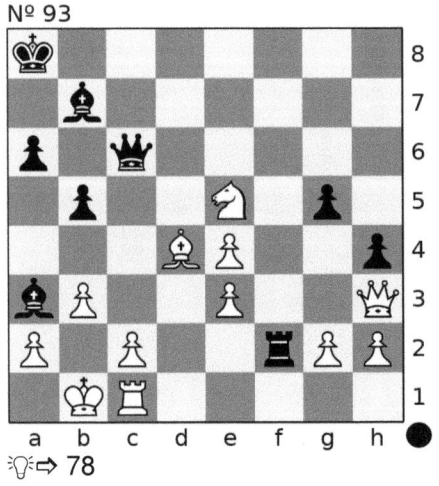

a b c d e f g h ●
💡⇨ 78

№ 94

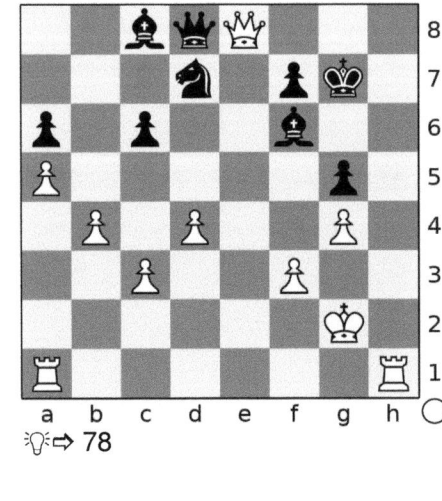

a b c d e f g h ○
💡⇨ 78

№ 95

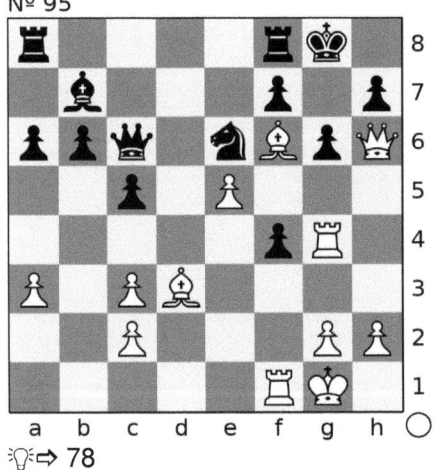

a b c d e f g h ○
💡⇨ 78

№ 96

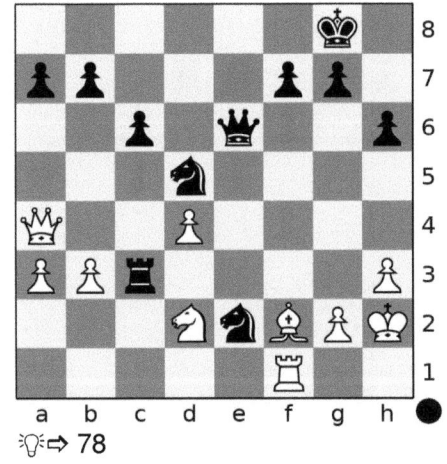

a b c d e f g h ●
💡⇨ 78

in 3

№ 97

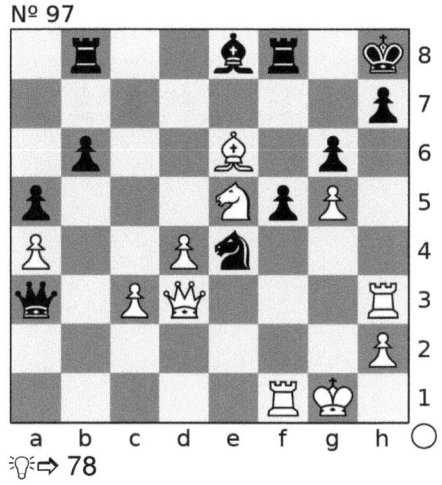

a b c d e f g h ○
💡⇨ 78

№ 98

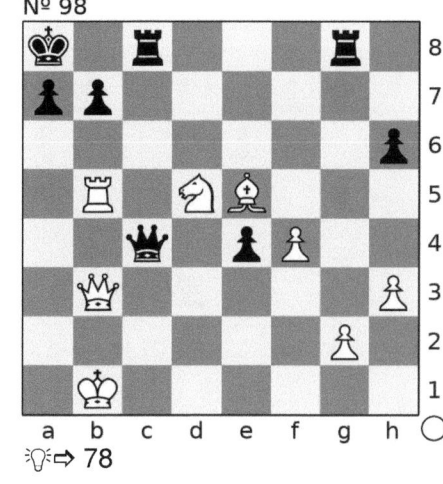

a b c d e f g h ○
💡⇨ 78

№ 99

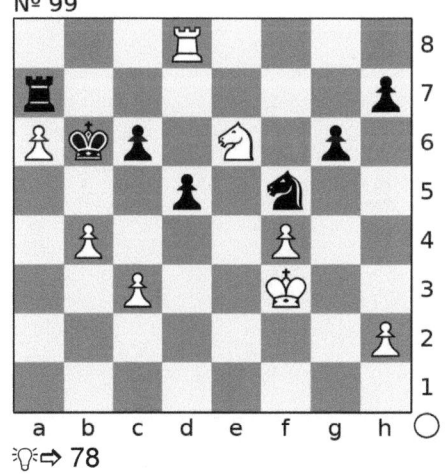

a b c d e f g h ○
💡⇨ 78

№ 100

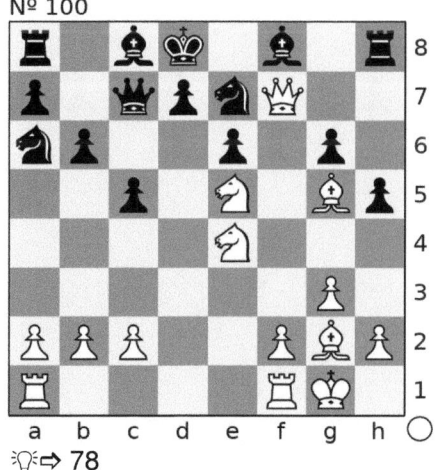

a b c d e f g h ○
💡⇨ 78

in 3

№ 101

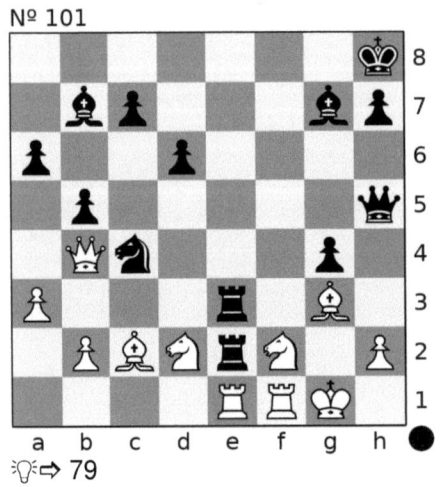

🔆⇨ 79

№ 102

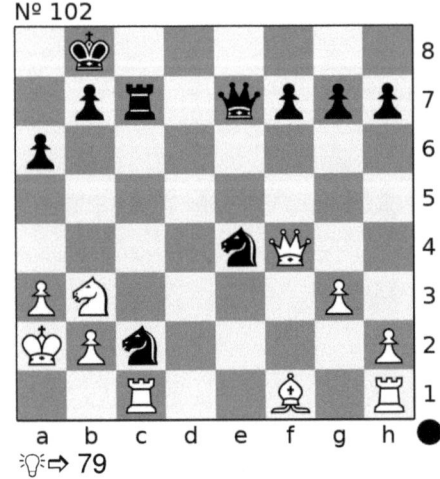

🔆⇨ 79

№ 103

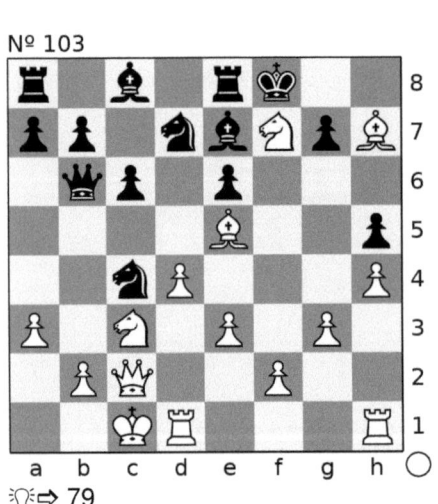

🔆⇨ 79

№ 104

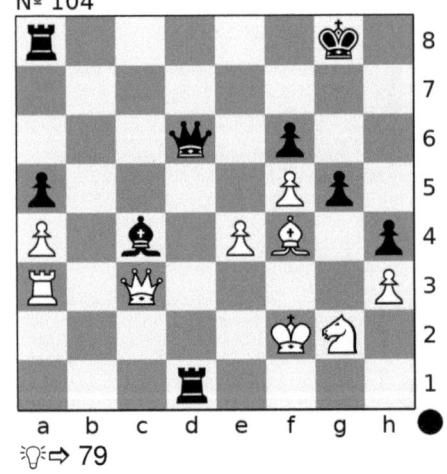

🔆⇨ 79

in 3

№ 105

a b c d e f g h ○

💡⇨ 79

№ 106

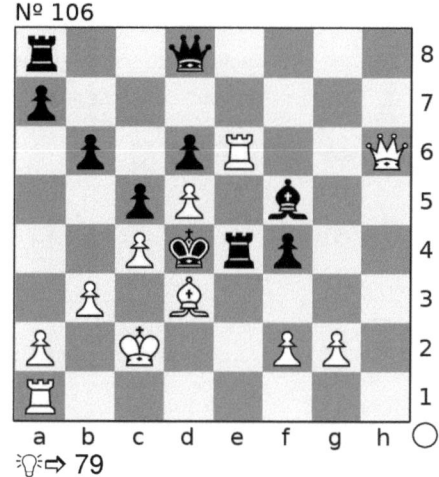

a b c d e f g h ○

💡⇨ 79

№ 107

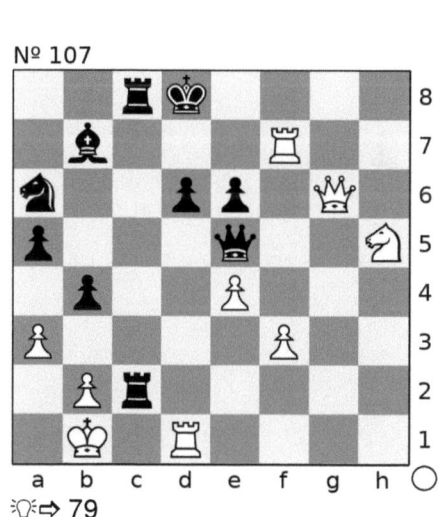

a b c d e f g h ○

💡⇨ 79

№ 108

a b c d e f g h ●

💡⇨ 79

in 3

№ 109

a b c d e f g h

💡⇨ 79

№ 110

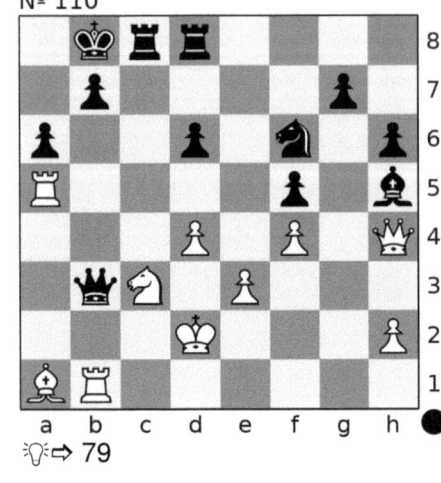

a b c d e f g h ●

💡⇨ 79

№ 111

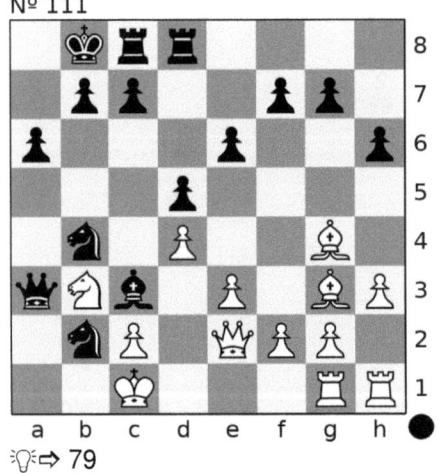

a b c d e f g h ●

💡⇨ 79

№ 112

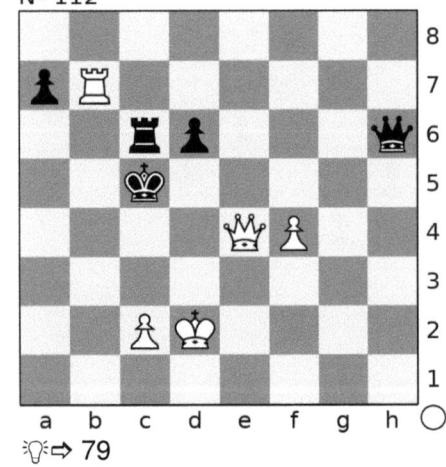

a b c d e f g h ○

💡⇨ 79

in 3

№ 113

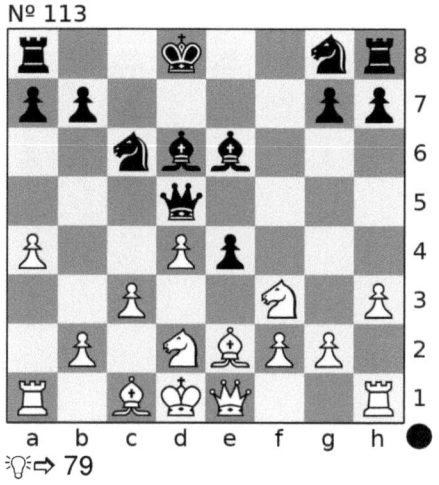

💡⇨ 79

№ 114

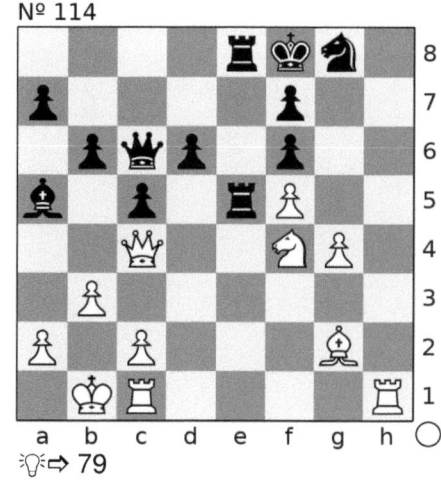

💡⇨ 79

№ 115

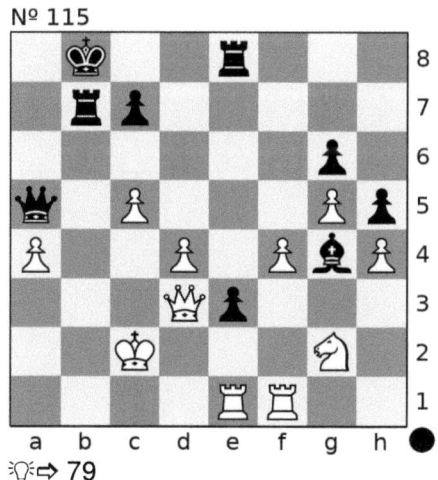

💡⇨ 79

№ 116

💡⇨ 79

in 3

№ 117

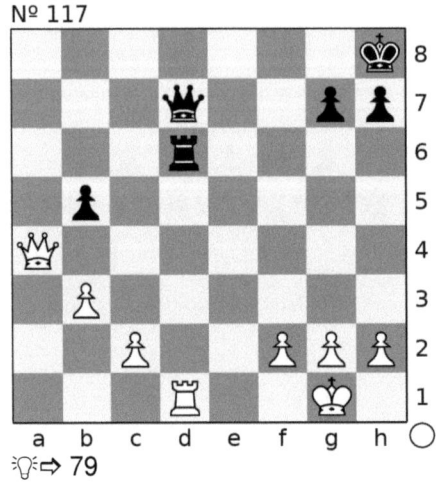

a b c d e f g h ○
💡⇨ 79

№ 118

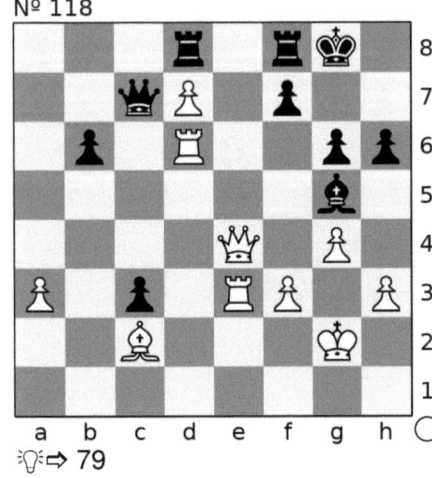

a b c d e f g h ○
💡⇨ 79

№ 119

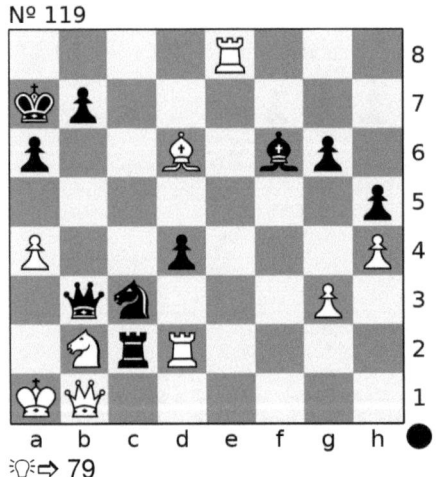

a b c d e f g h ●
💡⇨ 79

№ 120

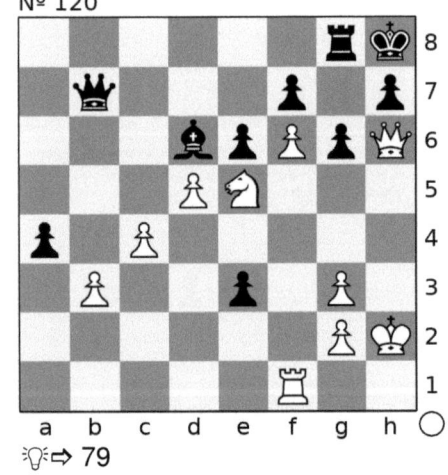

a b c d e f g h ○
💡⇨ 79

in 4

mate in four
mat en quatre
mate en cuatro
matt in vier
mat w czterech
mat in vier
mato en kwar

in 4

№ 121

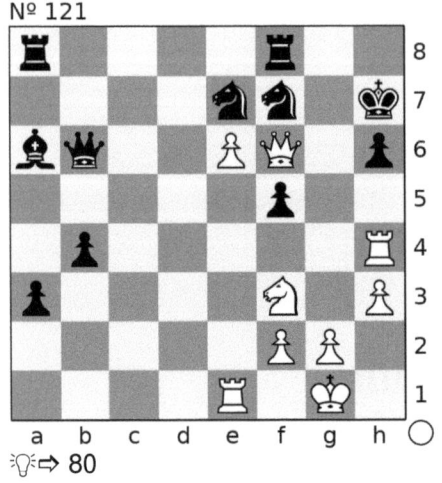

☀⇨ 80

№ 122

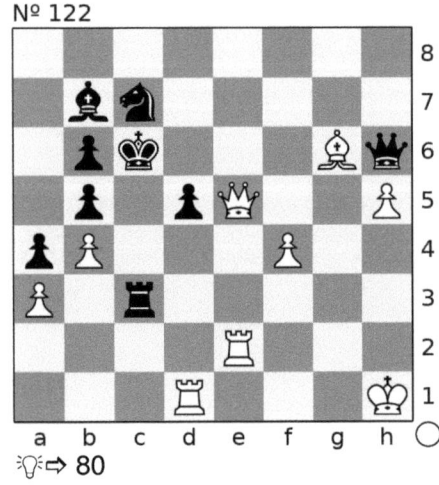

☀⇨ 80

№ 123

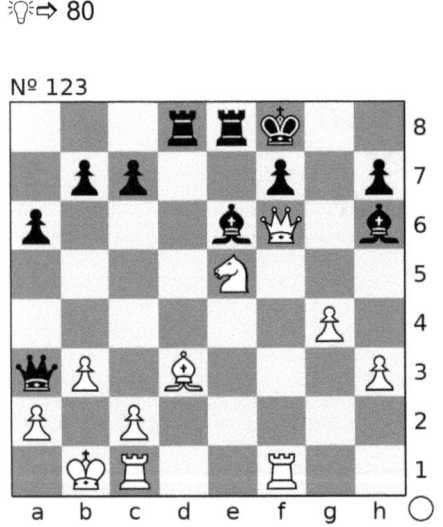

☀⇨ 80

№ 124

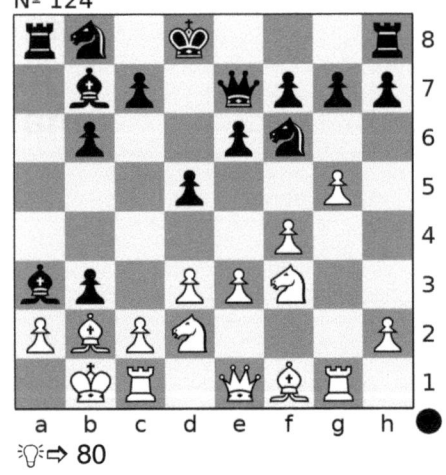

☀⇨ 80

№ 125

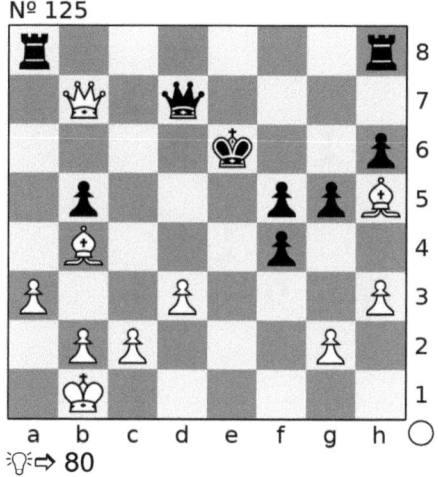

a b c d e f g h ○

💡⇨ 80

№ 126

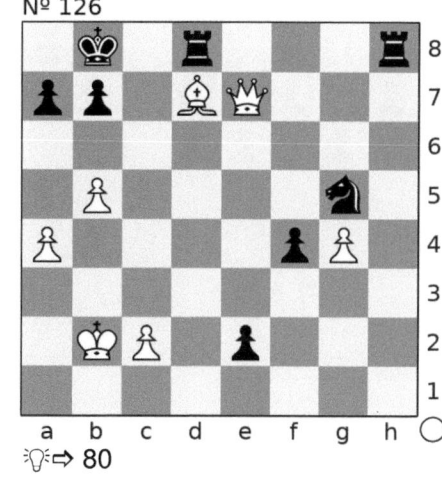

a b c d e f g h ○

💡⇨ 80

№ 127

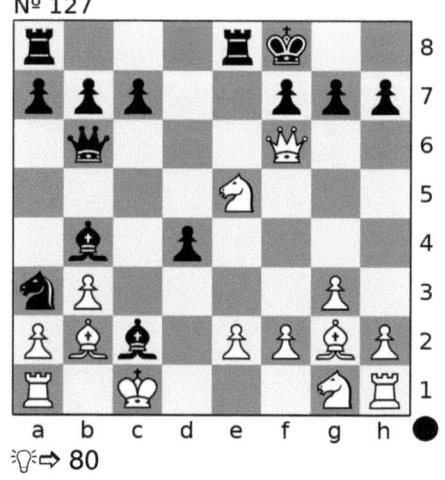

a b c d e f g h ●

💡⇨ 80

№ 128

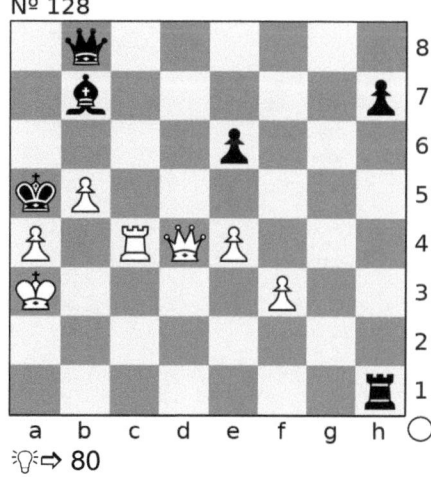

a b c d e f g h ○

💡⇨ 80

in 4

№ 129

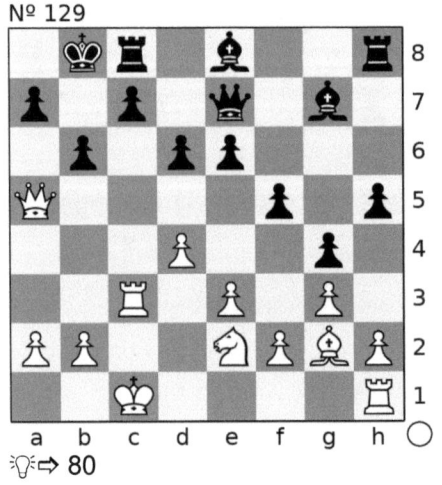

a b c d e f g h ○

№ 130

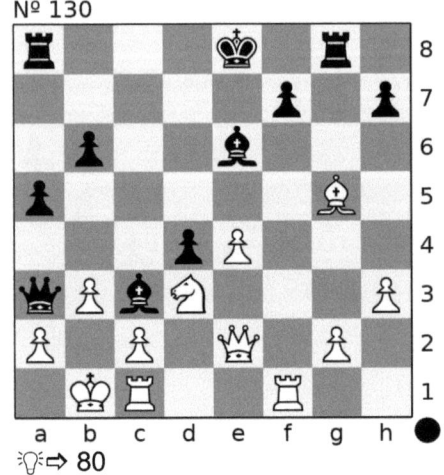

a b c d e f g h ●
💡⇨ 80

№ 131

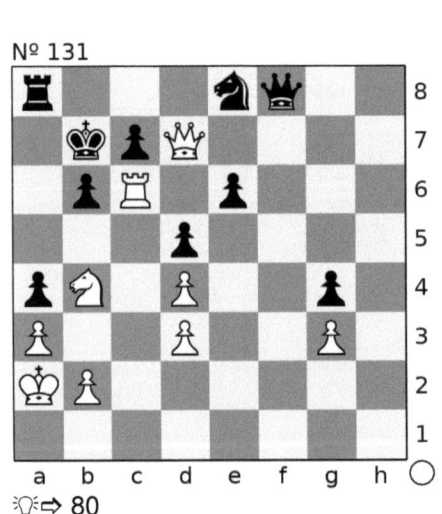

a b c d e f g h ○
💡⇨ 80

№ 132

a b c d e f g h ○
💡⇨ 80

№ 133

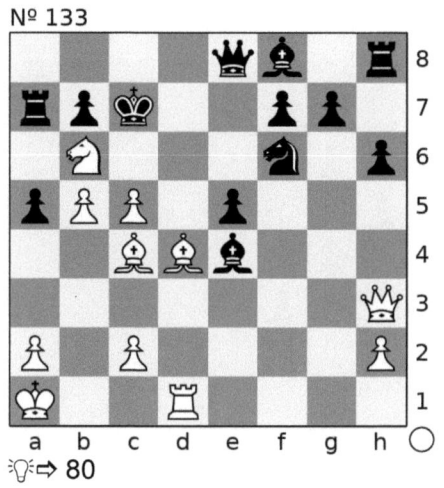

🔦⇨ 80

№ 134

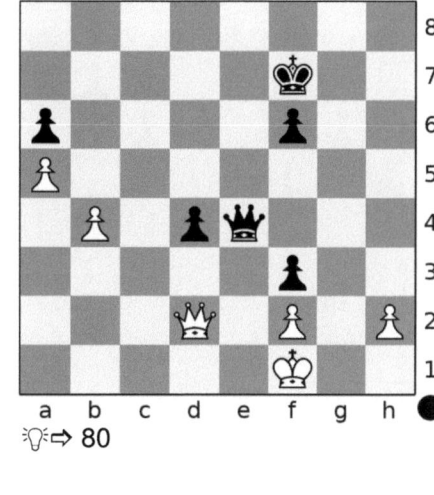

🔦⇨ 80

№ 135

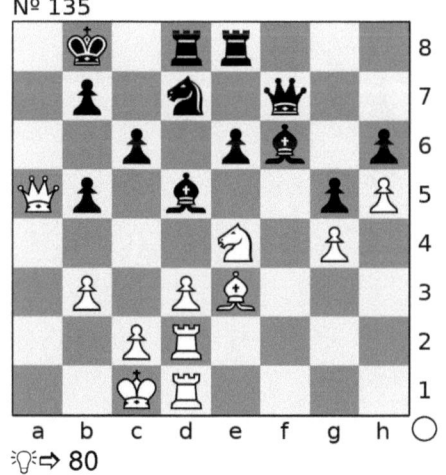

🔦⇨ 80

№ 136

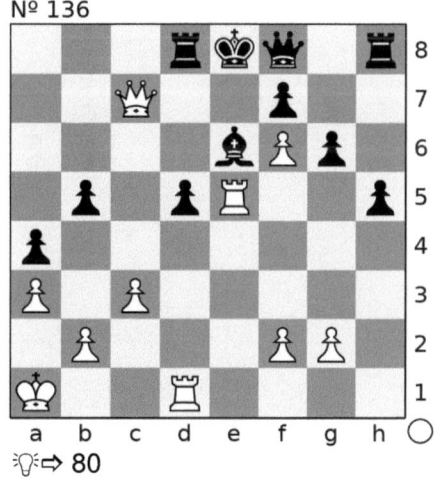

🔦⇨ 80

№ 137

a b c d e f g h ●

💡⇨ 80

№ 138

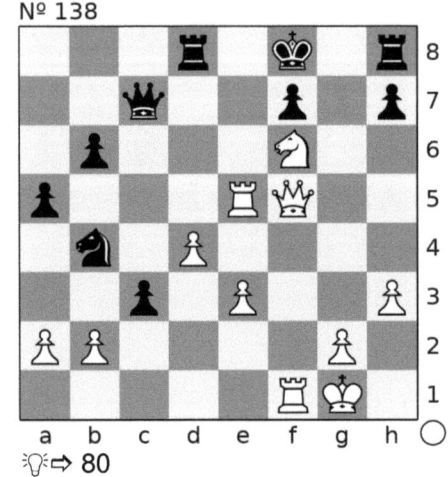

a b c d e f g h ○

💡⇨ 80

№ 139

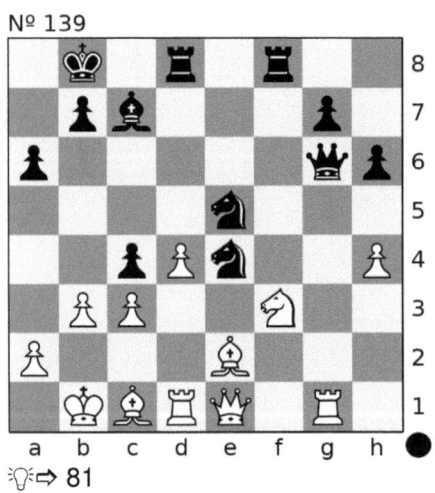

a b c d e f g h ●

💡⇨ 81

№ 140

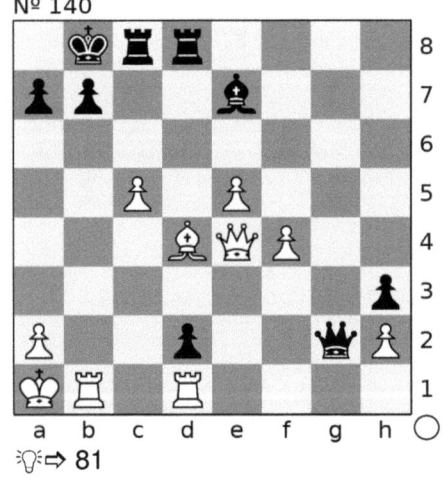

a b c d e f g h ○

💡⇨ 81

in 4

№ 141

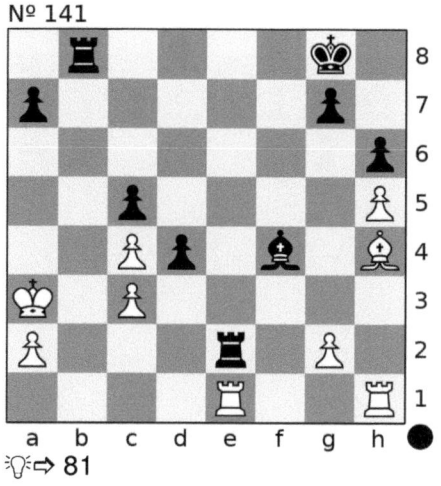

a b c d e f g h ●
⇒ 81

№ 142

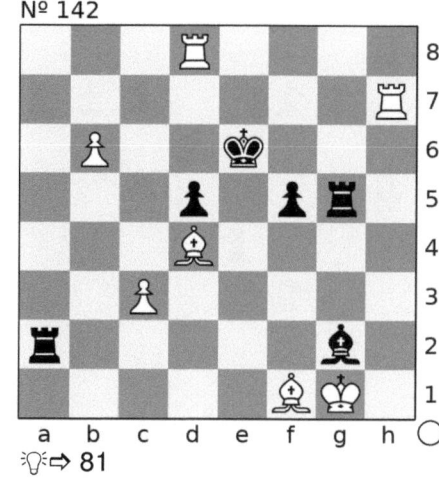

a b c d e f g h ○
⇒ 81

№ 143

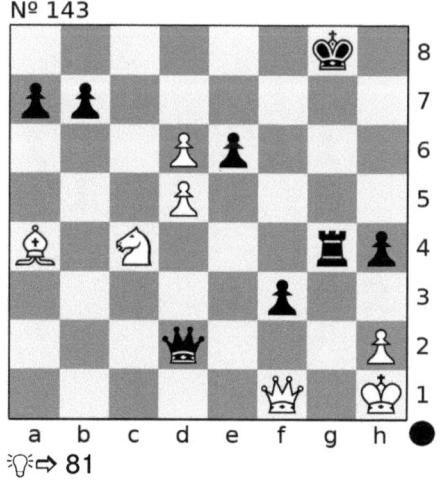

a b c d e f g h ●
⇒ 81

№ 144

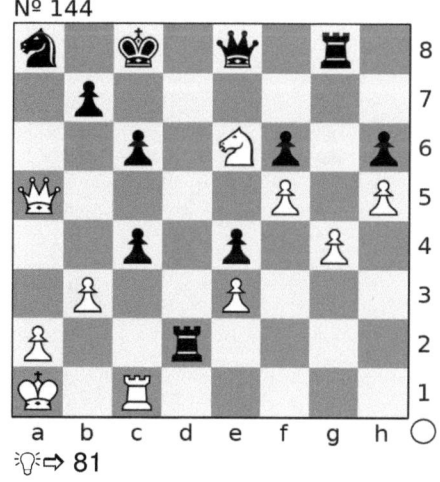

a b c d e f g h ○
⇒ 81

in 4

№ 145

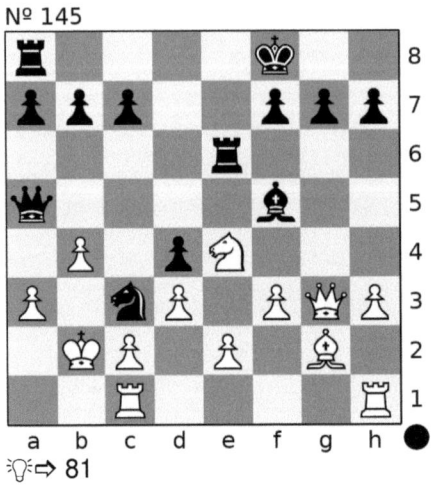

a b c d e f g h ●
🔅⇨ 81

№ 146

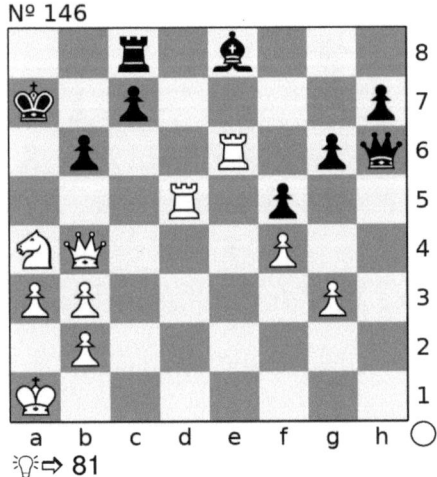

a b c d e f g h ○
🔅⇨ 81

№ 147

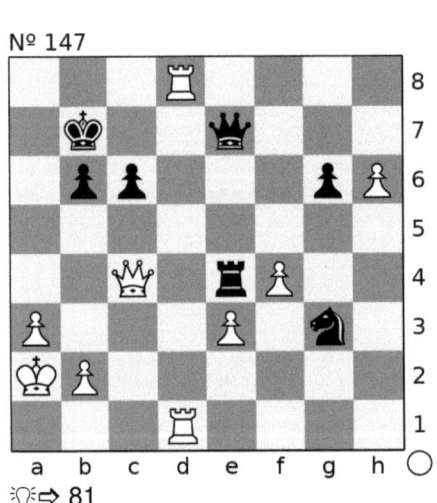

a b c d e f g h ○
🔅⇨ 81

№ 148

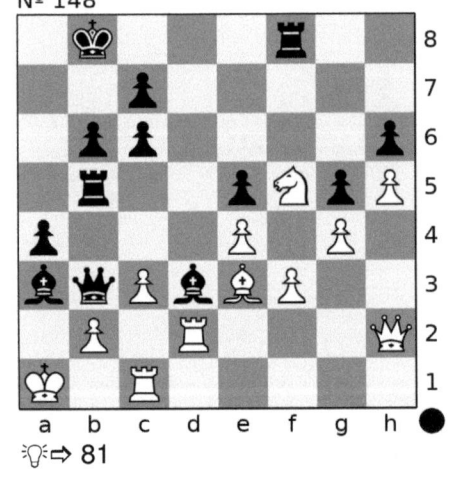

a b c d e f g h ●
🔅⇨ 81

№ 149

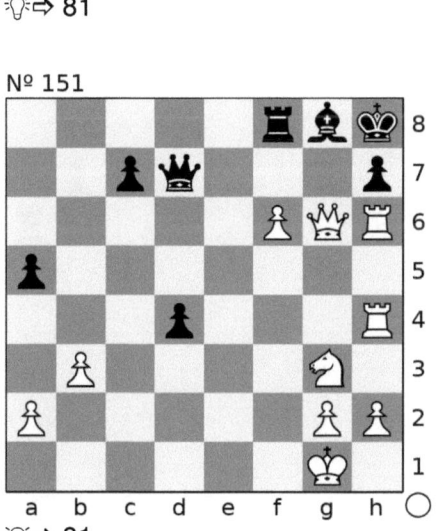

☝⇨ 81

№ 150

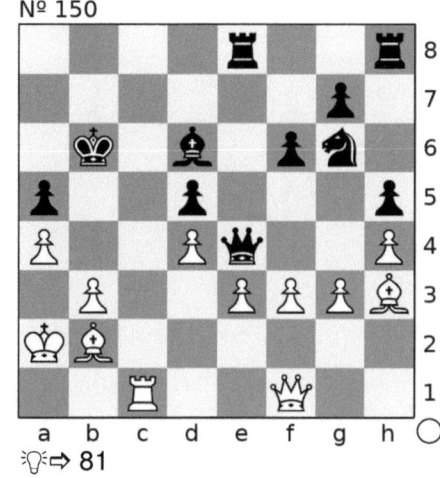

☝⇨ 81

№ 151

☝⇨ 81

№ 152

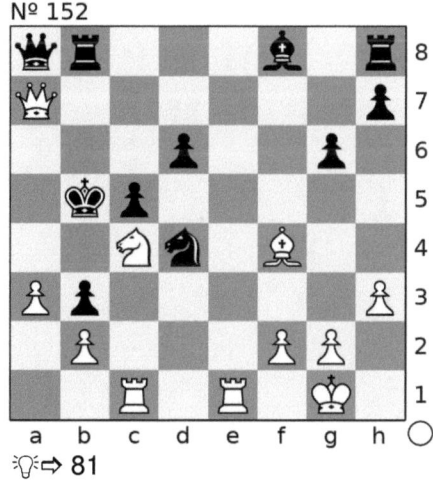

☝⇨ 81

in 4

№ 153

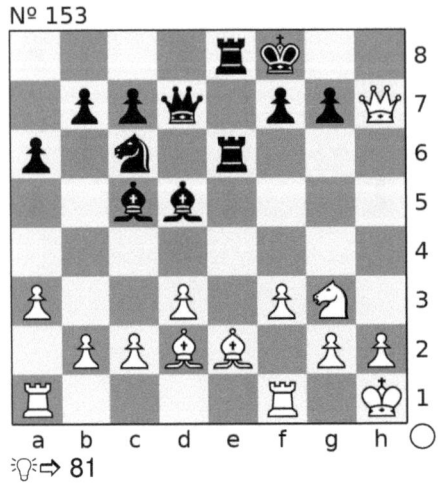

-☼-⇨ 81

№ 154

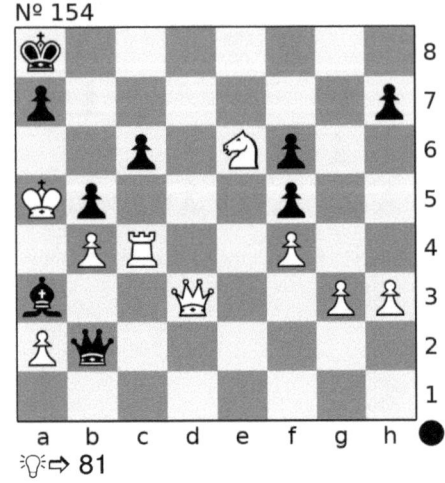

-☼-⇨ 81

№ 155

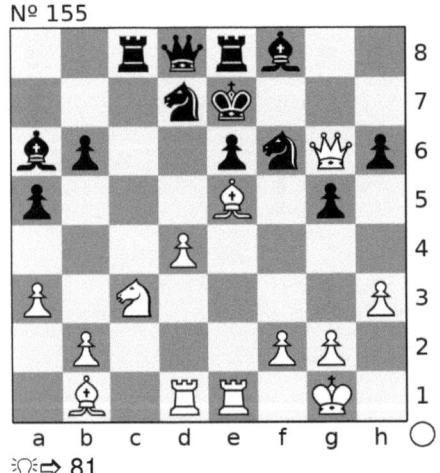

-☼-⇨ 81

№ 156

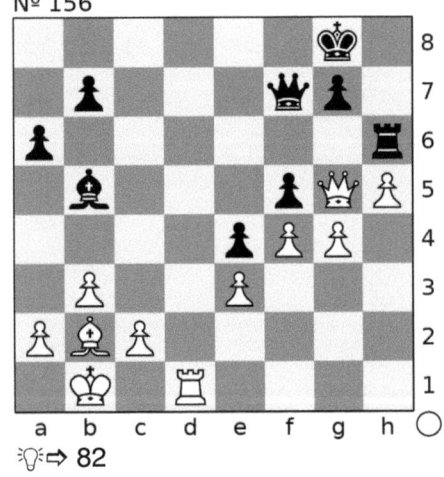

-☼-⇨ 82

in 4

№ 157

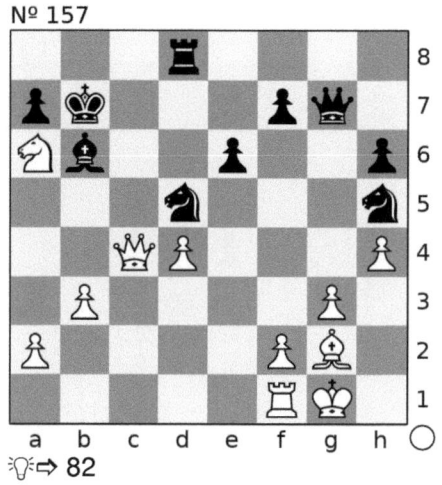

a b c d e f g h ○
💡⇨ 82

№ 158

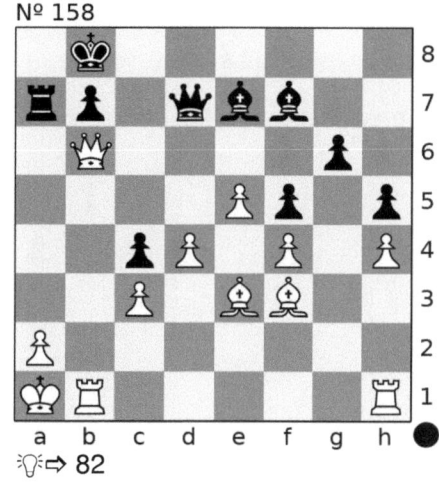

a b c d e f g h ●
💡⇨ 82

№ 159

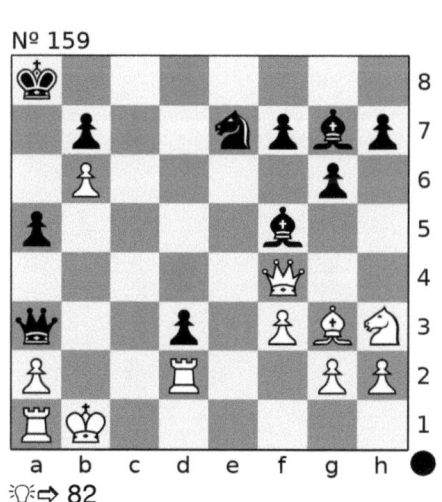

a b c d e f g h ●
💡⇨ 82

№ 160

a b c d e f g h ○
💡⇨ 82

in 4

№ 161

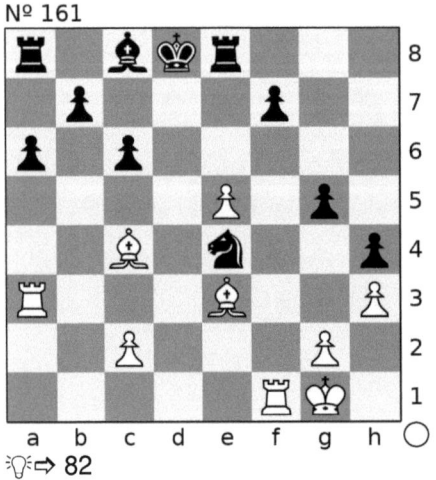

a b c d e f g h ○

🔆⇨ 82

№ 162

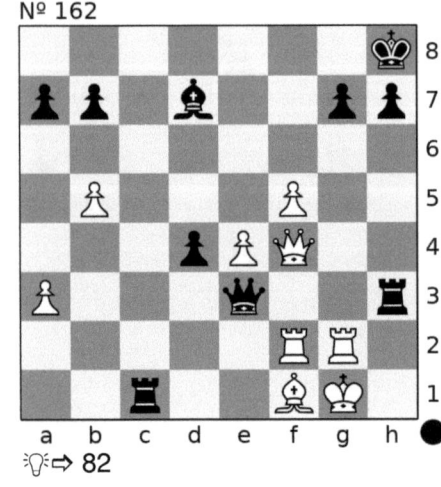

a b c d e f g h ●

🔆⇨ 82

№ 163

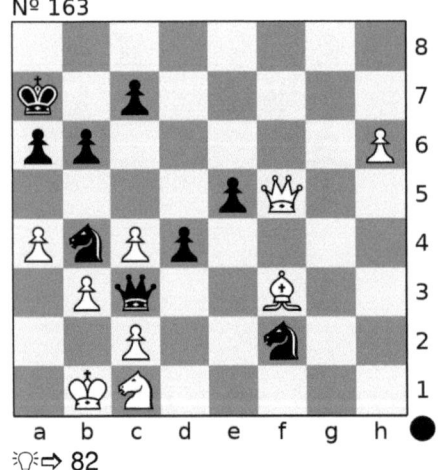

a b c d e f g h ●

🔆⇨ 82

№ 164

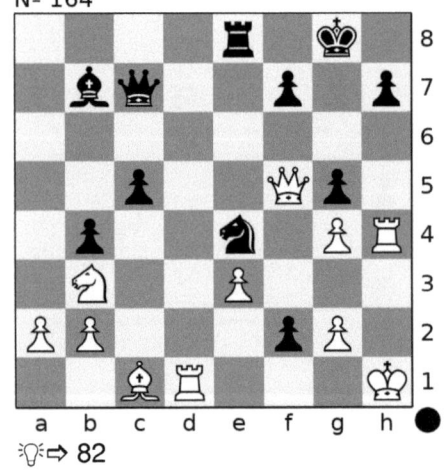

a b c d e f g h ●

🔆⇨ 82

in 4

№ 165

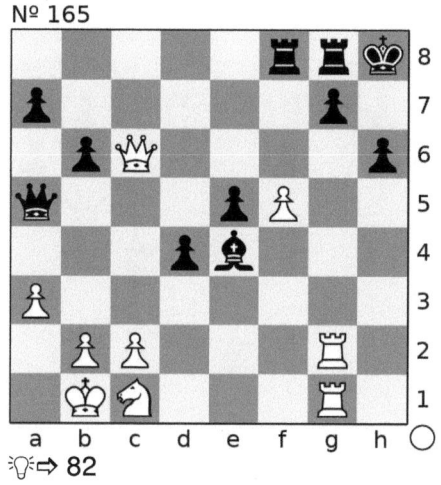

a b c d e f g h ○
🔆⇨ 82

№ 166

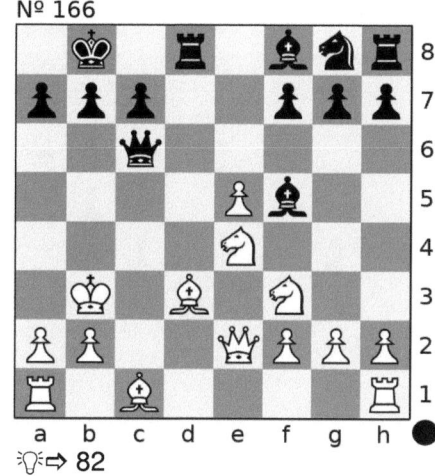

a b c d e f g h ●
🔆⇨ 82

№ 167

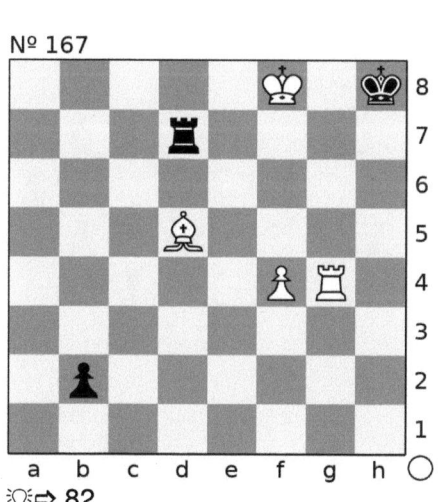

a b c d e f g h ○
🔆⇨ 82

№ 168

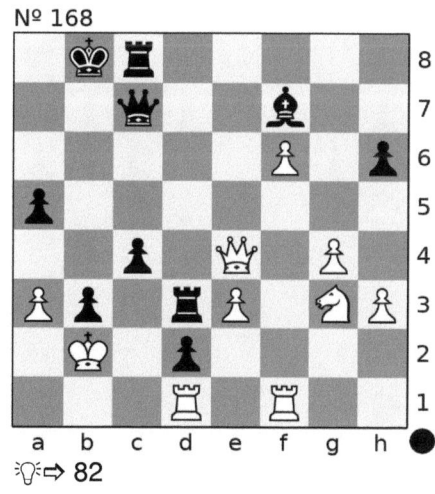

a b c d e f g h ●
🔆⇨ 82

in 4

№ 169

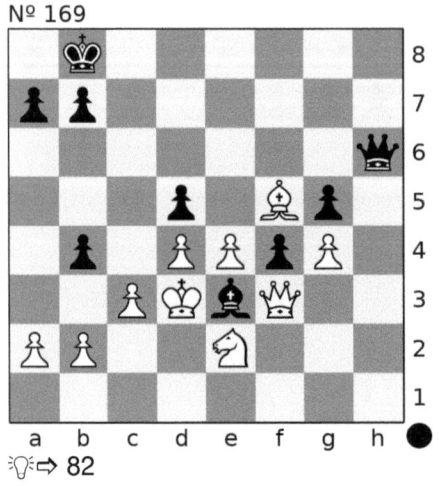

a b c d e f g h ●

💡⇨ 82

№ 170

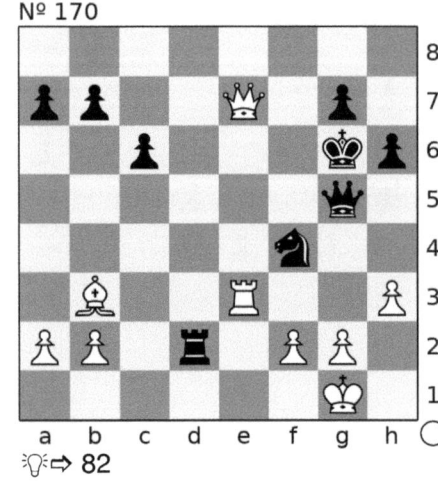

a b c d e f g h ○

💡⇨ 82

№ 171

a b c d e f g h ○

💡⇨ 82

№ 172

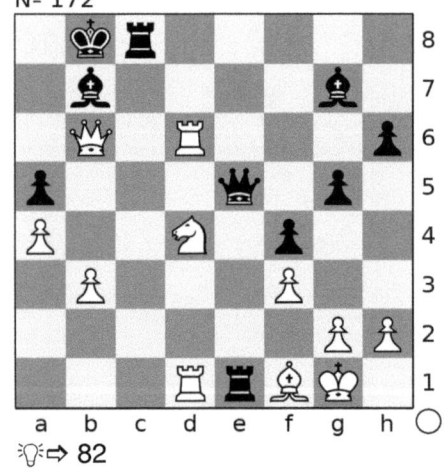

a b c d e f g h ○

💡⇨ 82

in 4

№ 173

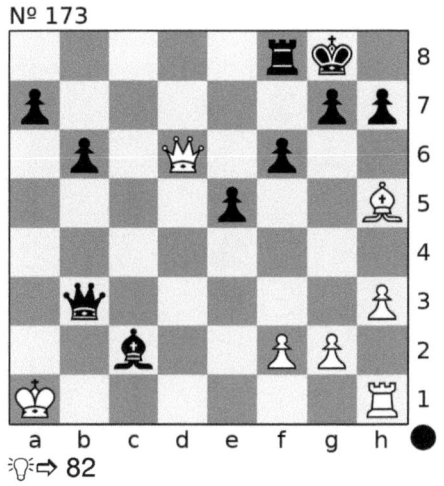

a b c d e f g h ●
💡⇨ 82

№ 174

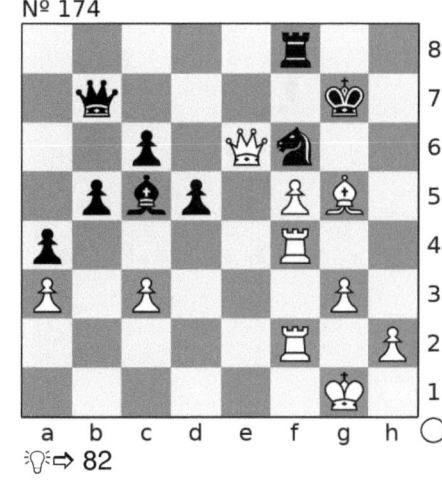

a b c d e f g h ○
💡⇨ 82

№ 175

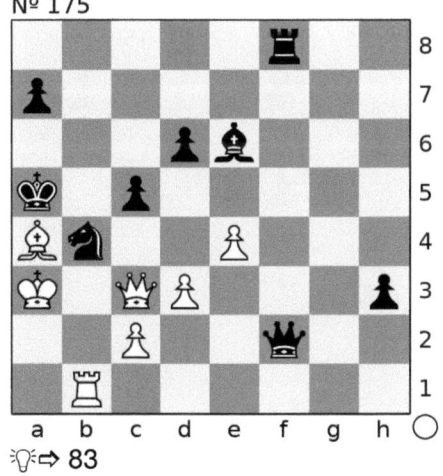

a b c d e f g h ○
💡⇨ 83

№ 176

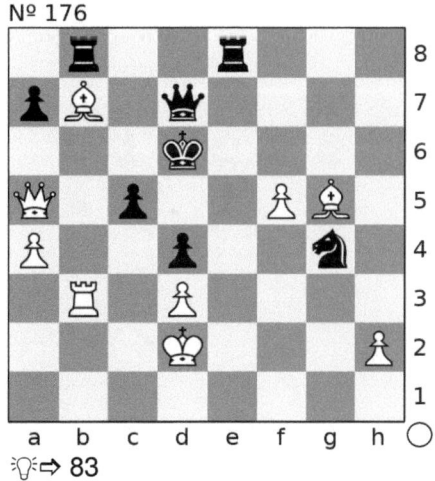

a b c d e f g h ○
💡⇨ 83

in 4

№ 177

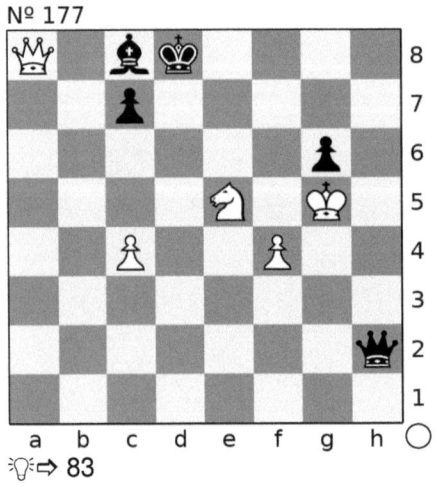

a b c d e f g h
💡⇨ 83

№ 178

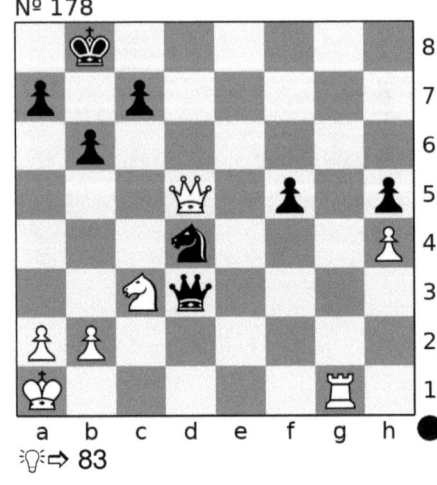

a b c d e f g h ●
💡⇨ 83

№ 179

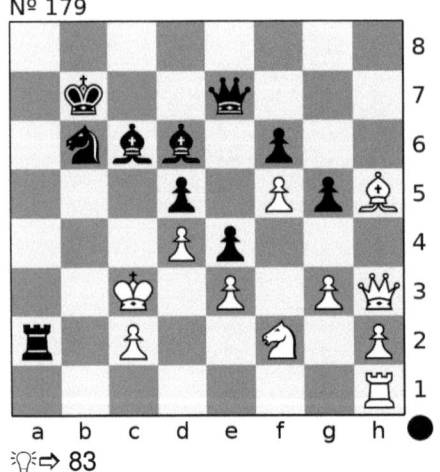

a b c d e f g h ●
💡⇨ 83

№ 180

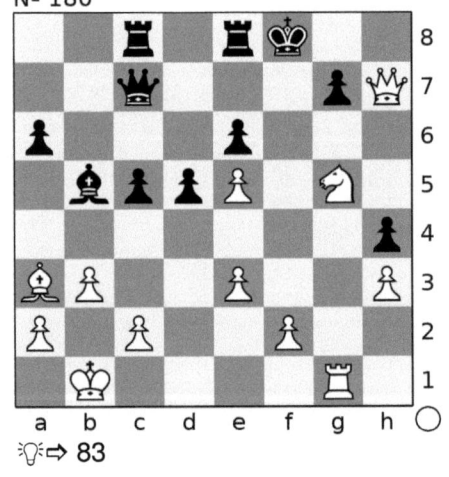

a b c d e f g h ○
💡⇨ 83

in 5

mate in five
mat en cinq
mate en cinco
matt in fünf
mat w pięciu
mat in vijf
mato en kvin

in 5

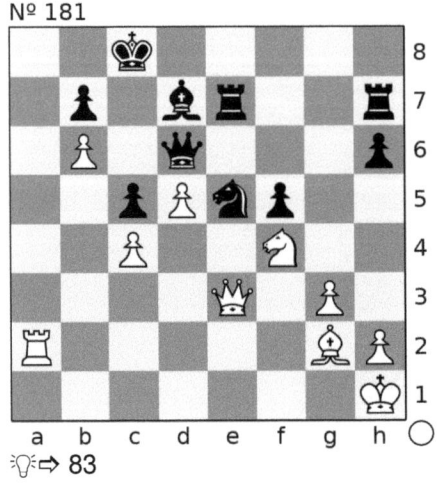

a b c d e f g h ○

💡⇨ 83

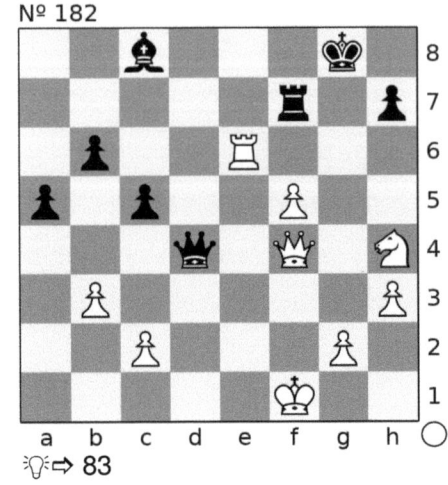

a b c d e f g h ○

💡⇨ 83

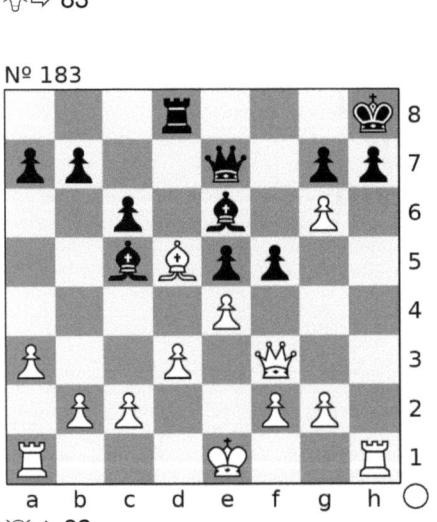

a b c d e f g h ○

💡⇨ 83

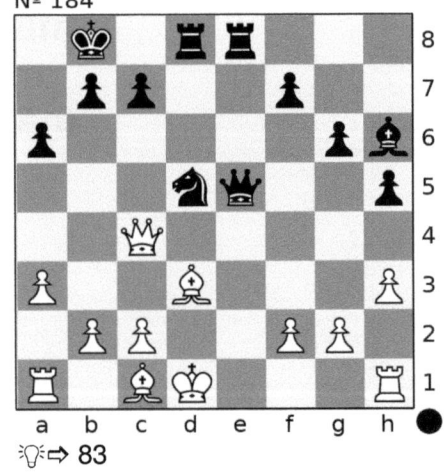

a b c d e f g h ●

💡⇨ 83

in 5

№ 185

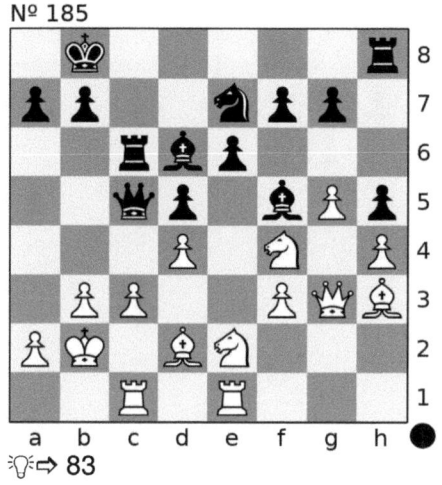

🔅⇨ 83

№ 186

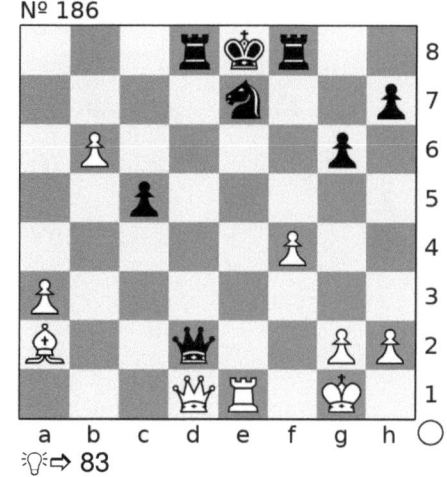

🔅⇨ 83

№ 187

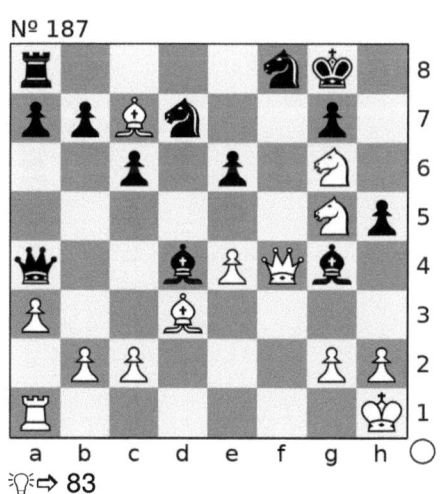

🔅⇨ 83

№ 188

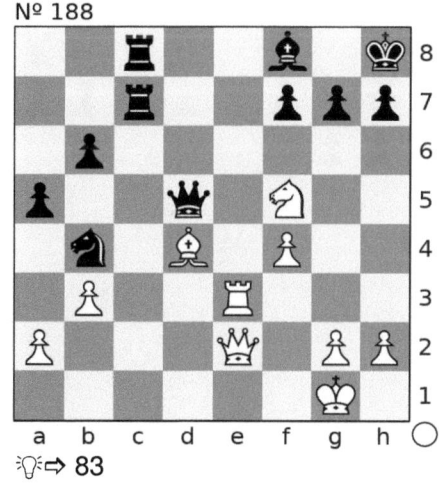

🔅⇨ 83

№ 189

⇨ 83

№ 190

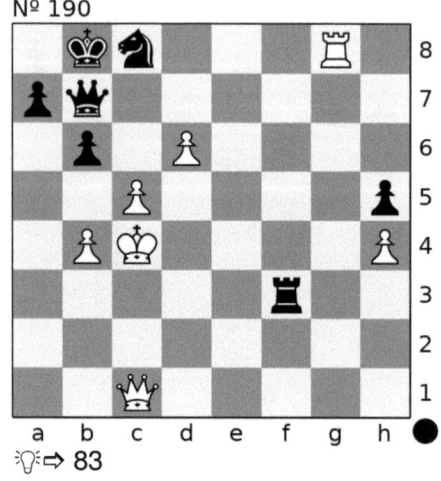

⇨ 83

№ 191

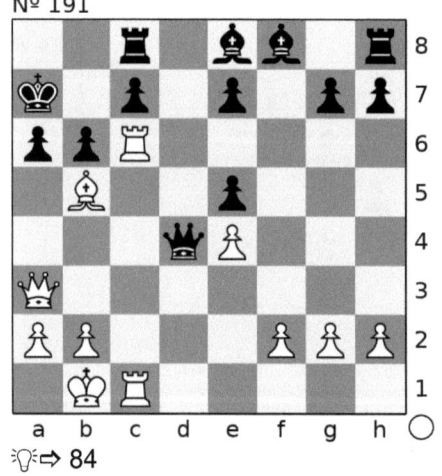

⇨ 84

№ 192

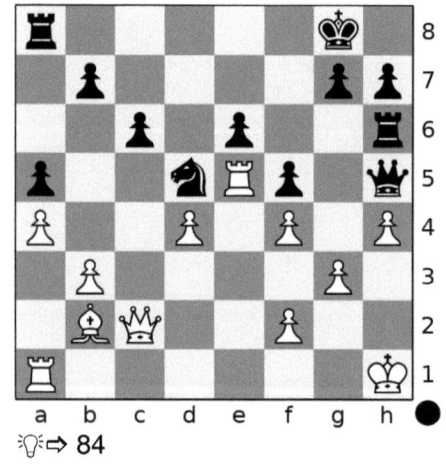

⇨ 84

№ 193

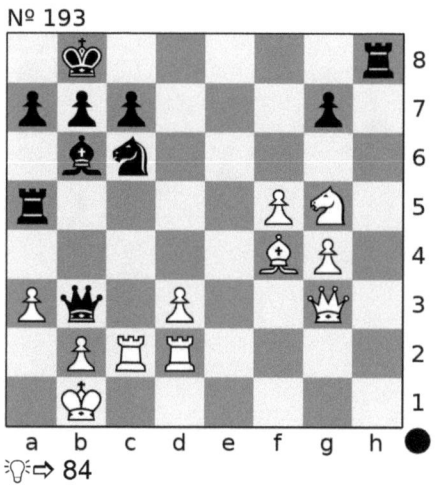

a b c d e f g h ●
💡⇨ 84

№ 194

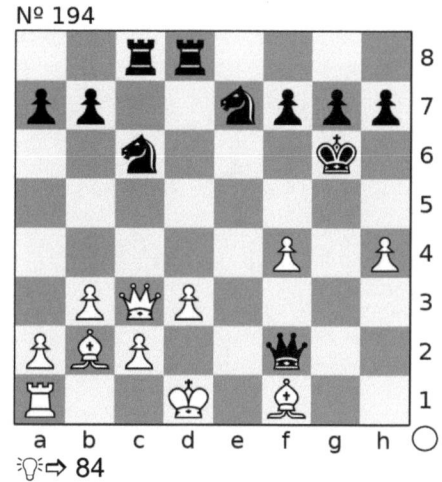

a b c d e f g h ○
💡⇨ 84

№ 195

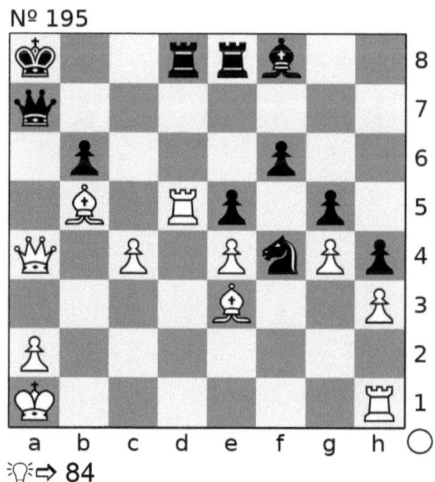

a b c d e f g h ○
💡⇨ 84

№ 196

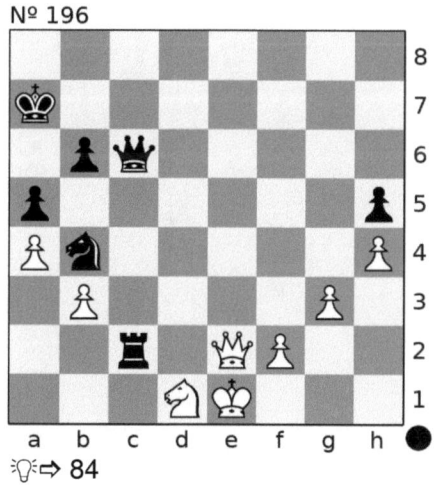

a b c d e f g h ●
💡⇨ 84

in 5

№ 197

⇨ 84

№ 198

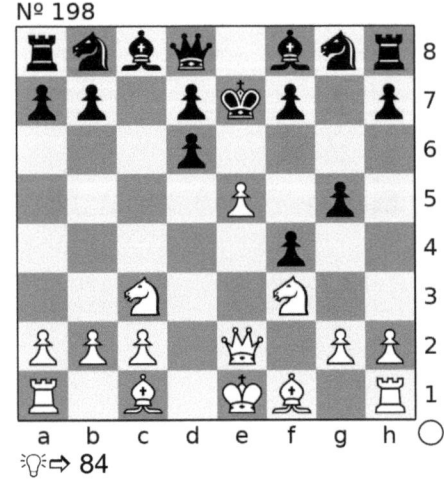

⇨ 84

№ 199

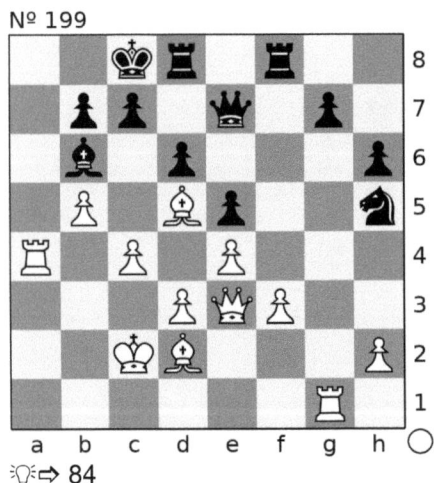

⇨ 84

№ 200

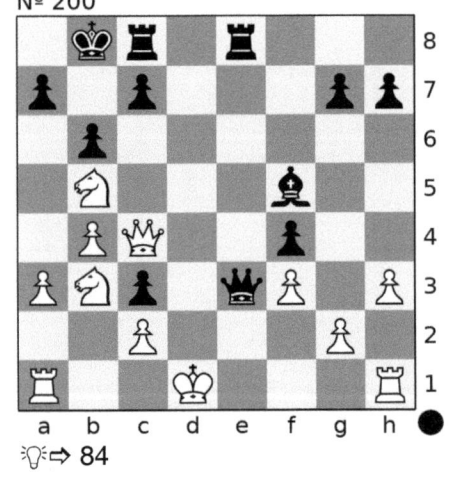

⇨ 84

# in 6

mate in six
mat en six
mate en seis
matt in sechs
mat w sześciu
mat in zes
mato en ses

in 6

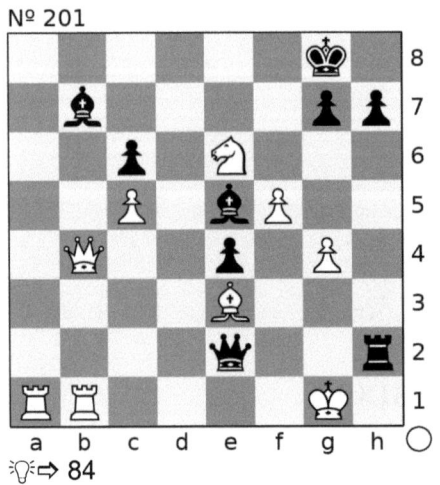

🔆⇨ 84

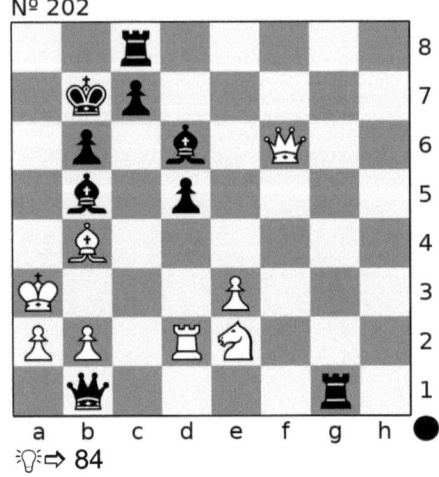

🔆⇨ 84

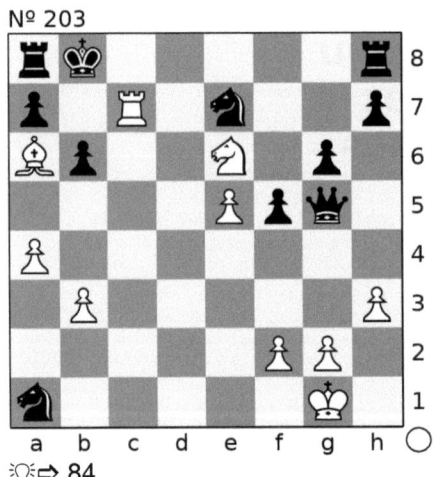

🔆⇨ 84

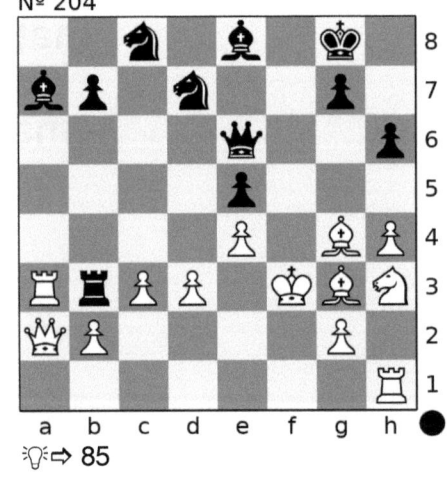

🔆⇨ 85

in 6

№ 205

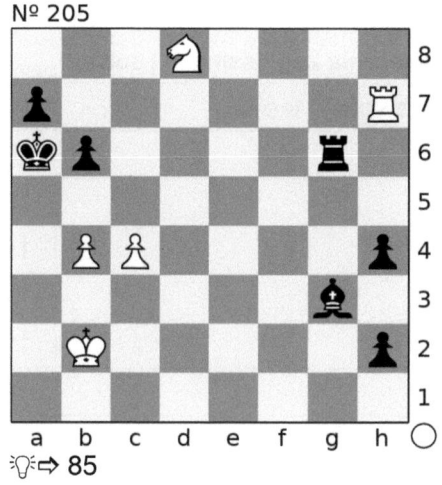

a b c d e f g h ○
💡⇨ 85

№ 206

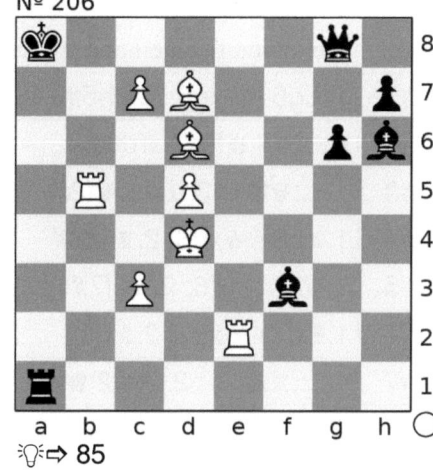

a b c d e f g h ○
💡⇨ 85

№ 207

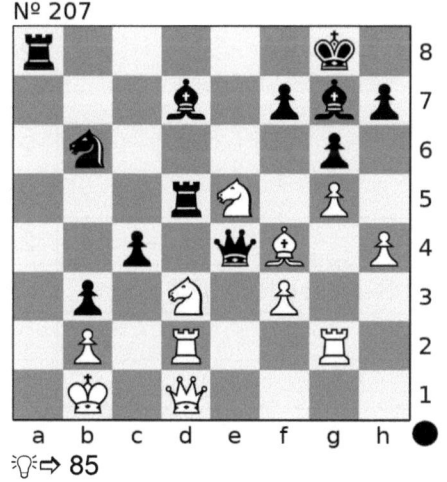

a b c d e f g h ●
💡⇨ 85

№ 208

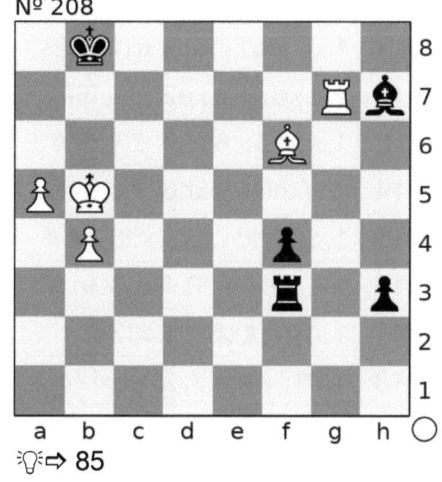

a b c d e f g h ○
💡⇨ 85

?	solutions | soluciones | lösungen | rozwiązania | oplossingen | solvoj	
#1	1.♗g6+:♚xg6; 2.♕h5# alt: 1.♗g6+:♜xg6; 2.♕e7#	18
#2	1.♗c4+:♚f6; 2.♕d6#	18
#3	1. ...:♛f1+; 2.♗xf1:♞f2#	18
#4	1.♜b8+:♚xb8; 2.♜xc8#	18
#5	1.♘f6+: gxf6; 2.♗+f7#	19
#6	1.♕d7+:♚xd7; 2.♗b5#	19
#7	1. ...:♜xa2+; 2.♔xa2:♛a5#	19
#8	1.♘g6+:♜xg6; 2.♕h7#	19
#9	1. ...:♕g2+; 2.♔xg2: h8=♕#	20
#10	1.♕h7+:♚xh7; 2. hxg6#	20
#11	1. ...:♕g1+; 2.♜xg1:♞f2#	20
#12	1.♘xd7+:♞xe2; 2.♘f6#	20
#13	1.♗xh5+:♛xh5; 2.♕d7#	21
#14	1.♕xh6+:♚xh6; 2.♜h4#	21
#15	1. ...:♟d8+; 2.♜xd8: b6#	21
#16	1. ...:♕h3+; 2.♗xh3:♞f3# alt: 1. ...:♕h3+; 2.♔g1:♕xg2#	21
#17	1.♜g7:♜c8*; 2.♜f3#	22
#18	1.♕f7+:♜xf7; 2. e6xf7#	22
#19	1. ...:♜h3+; 2. gxh3:♕f3#	22
#20	1. ...:♟b5+; 2. c4:♜d2#	22

?	solutions | soluciones | lösungen | rozwiązania | oplossingen | solvoj	📄
#21	1. ...:♟d2+; 2.♕f4*:♛g4#	23
#22	1. ...:♞d3+; 2.♖xd3:♝f2#	23
#23	1.♖e8+:♝xe8; 2. ♕c3#	23
#24	1. ...:♛xe3+; 2.♔xe3:♝xf4#	23
#25	1.♕xf7+:♜xf7; 2.♖e8#	24
#26	1.♕xc6+:bxc6; 2.♗a6#	24
#27	1.♖xf6+:♜xf6; 2. g5#	24
#28	1. ...:♕g1+; 2.♖xg1:♞g3#	24
#29	1.♕h7+:♚xf6; 2.♘e4#	25
#30	1. b2+:♔b1; 2.♞c3#	25
#31	1.♗d6+:♕xd6*; 2.♕f7#	25
#32	1. ...:♝xd3+; 2.♔e1:♛f3#	25
#33	1. ...:♞e4+; 2.♔e2:♛d2#	26
#34	1.♖h6+:♚xg5; 2.♕h4#	26
#35	1.♕c6:♚xa6; 2.♕a8# alt: 1.♕c6:♚b8*; 2.♕b7#	26
#36	1.♕g7+:♝xg7; 2.♖d8# alt: 1.♕g7+:♚e8; 2.♕g8#	26
#37	1.♖d5+:♚xd5; 2.♕e5#	27
#38	1. ...:♜c1+; 2.♕xc1:♚e2#	27
#39	1. ...:♜g2+; 2.♔h3*:♜h2#	27
#40	1.♖xh6+:♚xh6; 2.♕xh4# alt: 1.♖xh6+:♚g8; 2.♕a8#	27

75

?	solutions | soluciones | lösungen | rozwiązania | oplossingen | solvoj	🗎
#41	1.♗f6+:♔xf6; 2.♘g8# alt: 1. ...:♔xh6; 2.♕g5# | 1.♗h4+:♔h8; 2.♕g8#	28
#42	1.♗f6+:♞xf6*; 2.♕c7#	28
#43	1.♕xe6+: fxe6; 2.♗g6# alt: 1. ...: ♗fe7; 2.♕xe7#	28
#44	1. ...:♕h5+; 2.♔f6:♕f5#	28
#45	1. ...:♞b3+; 2. axb3:♕a5#	29
#46	1.♕g8+:♜xg8; 2.♘f7#	29
#47	1.♘xb6+: cxb6*; 2.♕c8#	29
#48	1. ...:♗e4+; 2.♔c3:♕xe3#	29
#49	1.♕f8+:♔xf8; 2.♖d8# alt: 1. ...:♔h7; 2.♕g7#	30
#50	1. ...:♕a1+; 2.♕xa1:♜c3#	30
#51	1.♕h7+:♔xf6; 2.♘d5#	30
#52	1.♖xe8+:♗xe8; 2.♕f8# alt: 1....:♔g7; 2.♕f8# | 1....:♕xe8; 2.♕f6#	30
#53	1.♕g4+:♗xg4;♗f7#	31
#54	1.♕g6+: hxg6; 2. fxg6#	31
#55	1.♕f8+:♔xf8; 2.♖h8#	31
#56	1. ...:♗xg2+; 2.♔xg2: h1=♕#	31
#57	1.♘f6+:gxf6; 2.♗f7#	32
#58	1.♗e1+:♜xe1; 2. g7#	32
#59	1.♕h8+:♔xh8; 2.♖e8# alt: 1.♕h8+:♔f7; 2.♕g7#	32
#60	1.♖xa6+: bxa6; 2.♕c6#	32

?	solutions | soluciones | lösungen | rozwiązania | oplossingen | solvoj	🖹
#61	1.♘g5+: hxg5; 2.♕h5+:♚g8; 3.♖e8#	34
#62	1.♕xe6:♞e7; 2.♕g8+:♞xg8; 3.♘f7#	34
#63	1. ...:♜f1+; 2.♘f2:♜xf2+; 3.♕xf2:♕e4#	34
#64	1.♕xg6+:♞xg6; 2.♖g8+:♚h7; 3. hxg6#	34
#65	1.♕xd7+:♚xd7; 2.♘b6+:♚e8; 3.♗a4#	35
#66	1.♖xg5+: ♜f5; 2.♖xf5+:♗c5; 3.♗d2# alt: 2. ...: b5; 3.♗c7#	35
#67	1.♘g6+:♚xh7; 2.♘xf8+:♚g8*; 3.♕h7#	35
#68	1.♗h6+:♚h8; 2.♖xf8+:♜xf8; 3.♖xf8#	35
#69	1. ...:♞4c3+; 2. bxc3:♗a3+; 3. axb5:♞c3#	36
#70	1.♕xg6+: fxg6; 2.♘g5+: hxg5; 3. hxg6#	36
#71	1.♖xc6+:♛d8; 2.♕xb8+:♚e7; 3.♕d6#	36
#72	1.♕d8+:♚xd8; 2.♗a5+:♚e8; 3.♖d8#	36
#73	1.♔b1:♗xe4; 2. d4:♜xc8*; 3. a3#	37
#74	1. ...:♞e2+; 2.♔h1:♞g3+; 3.♔g1:♜xf1#	37
#75	1.♘xg7+:♛d8; 2.♕f6+:♞xf6; 3.♗c7#	37
#76	1.♖e8+:♜xe8; 2.♖xe8+:♚h2*; 3.♕g6#	37
#77	1. ...:♗b2+; 2.♔xa2:♗xc2+; 3.♗xa8:♜xa8#	38
#78	1.♕f7+:♚h8; 2.♖xh6+: gxh6; 3.♕h7#	38
#79	1.♕g7+:♗xg7; 2. hxg7:♚g8; 3.♘h6#	38
#80	1. ...:♞f3+; 2.♔g2:♕g5+; 3.♔h3:♜h8#	38

?	solutions | soluciones | lösungen | rozwiązania | oplossingen | solvoj	📄
#81	1.♕g6: fxg6; 2.♖g7+:♚f8; 3.♘g6#	39
#82	1.♖b7+:♚xb7; 2.♕c6+:♚a6; 3.♕b6# alt: 2. ...:♚a5; 3.♘b6#	39
#83	1. ...:♛e1+; 2.♔a2:♝c4+; 3.♔xa3:♛xc3#	39
#84	1. ...:♞h3+; 2.♔g2:♛f2+; 3.♔xh3:♛f3#	39
#85	1.♖h6+; gxh6; 2.♕xh6+:♚f5; 3.♕g5#	40
#86	1.♖h8+:♝xh8; 2.♕h7+:♚f8; 3.♕f7#	40
#87	1.♖h7+:♚xh7; 2.♗h6+:♚xh6; 3.♕g5#	40
#88	1. ...:♛c1+:♗xc1; 2.♜xc1:♔e2; 3.♞f4#	40
#89	1.♗g7+:♚g8; 2.♕xe8+:♚h7; 3.♕h8#	41
#90	1. ...:♝f1; 2.♖xf1:♕xf1+; 3.♕xf1:♜xf1#	41
#91	1.♕d8+:♚b7; 2.♘c5+:♞xc5; 3.♕b8#	41
#92	1.♕c4+:♝e6; 2.♕f4+:♝f5; 3.♕xf5#	41
#93	1. ...:♛xc2+; 2.♖xc2:♜f1+; 3.♖c1:♜xc1#	42
#94	1.♖h7+:♚xh7; 2.♕xf7+:♚h8*; 3.♖h1#	42
#95	1.♕xh7+:♚xh7; 2.♖h4+:♚g8; 3.♖h8#	42
#96	1. ...:♜xh3+; 2. gxh3:♞df4; 3.♕xa7*:♕xh3#	42
#97	1.♖xh7+:♚xh7; 2.♕h3+:♚g7;3.♕h6#	43
#98	1.♘b6+: axb6; 2.♕a3+: ♛a4; 3.♕xa4#	43
#99	1.♖b8+:♜b7; 2.♖xb7+:♚xa6; 3.♘c5#	43
#100	1.♕e8+:♚xe8; 2.♘f6+:♚d8; 3.♘f7#	43

?	solutions | soluciones | lösungen | rozwiązania | oplossingen | solvoj	📄
#101	1. ...:♖xg3+; 2. hxg3:♛h8+; 3.♘xh8:♖g2#	44
#102	1. ...:♞c3+; 2. bxc3:♛xa3+; 3.♔b1:♛xb3#	44
#103	1. ♗xg7+:♚xg7; 2.♕g6+: ♚f8; 3.♕g8#	44
#104	1. ...:♖f1+; 2.♔e3:♛c5+; 3.♔d2:♛f2#	44
#105	1.♕xh8+:♚xh8; 2.♗f6+:♚g8; 3.♖e8#	45
#106	1.♖xe4+:♗xe4; 2.♕g7+:♛f6; 3.♕xf6#	45
#107	1.♖xd6:♛xd6; 2.♕f6:♚e8; 3.♘g7#	45
#108	1. ...:♞d3+; .♔h1:♛h2+; 3.♘xh2:♖xh2#	45
#109	1. ♖xf6+:♗xf6; 2.♕d7+:♚e5; 3.♕xd5#	46
#110	1. ...:♞e4+; 2.♔e1:♛xb1+; 3.♘xb1:♖c1#	46
#111	1. ...:♞7d3+; 2.♔d1:♛c1+; 3.♘xc1:♞b2#	46
#112	1.♕e3+:♚d5; 2.♖b5+:♚c4; 3.♕d3#	46
#113	1. ...:♛b3+; 2.♘xb3:♗xb3+; 3.♔d2:♗f4#	47
#114	1.♕xf7+:♚xf7; 2.♖h7+:♚f8; 3.♘g6#	47
#115	1. ...:♛xa4+; 2.♔c1:♛a1+; 3.♔c2:♛b2#	47
#116	1. ...:♛a3; 2.♕c8+:♗xc8*; 3.bxa3:♞xa3# alt: 3.♘xd4*:♛xa3#	47
#117	1.♕a8+:♛d8; 2.♕xd8+:♖xd8; 3.♖xd8#	48
#118	1.♖xg6+: fxg6; 2.♕xg6+:♚h8; 3.♕h7# alt: 1. ...:♚h8; 2.♖g8(h7)+:*	48
#119	1. ...:♛xa2+; 2.♕xa2:♖c1+; 3.♕b1:♖xb1#	48
#120	1.♖h1:e2*; 2.♕h7+:♚xh7; 3.♔g1#	48

?	solutions | soluciones | lösungen | rozwiązania | oplossingen | solvoj	📄
#121	1.♘g5+:♚g8; 2. exf7+:♜xf7; 3.♕xf7+:♚h8; 4.♕h7#	50
#122	1.♗e8+:♞xe8; 2.♕xd5+:♚c7; 3.♖e7+:♚c8*; 4.♕xb7#	50
#123	1.♕xf7+:♝xf7; 2.♖xf7+:♚g8; 3.♗xh7+:♚h8; 3.♘g6#	50
#124	1. ...: bxa2+; 2.♔a1:♝xb2+; 3.♔xb2:♛a3+; 4.♔a1:♛c3#	50
#125	1.♕b6+:♚d5; 2.♗f6+:♚e5; 3.♗c3+:♚d4; 4.♕xd4#	51
#126	1.♗c6: bxc6; 2. bxc6:♜d7; 3.♕xd7: e1=♕; 5.♕b7#	51
#127	1. ...:♝d2+; 2.♔xd2:♕b4+; 3.♗c3:♕xc3+; 4.♔c1:♝xb3#	51
#128	1.♕c3+:♚b6; 2.♖c6+:♗xc6; 3.♕xc6+:♚a5; 4.♕a6#	51
#129	1.♕xa7+:♚xa7; 2.♖a3+:♝a4; 3.♖xa4+:♚b8; 4.♖a8#	52
#130	1. ...: a4; 2.♕f3*:♕xa2+; 3.♔xa2: axb3+; 4.♔b1:♜a1#	52
#131	1.♖xb6+:♚xb6; 2.♕c6+:♚a5; 3.♕xa8+:♚b5; 4.♕a6# alt: 2. ...:♚a7; 3.♕a6+:♚b8; 4.♘c6#	52
#132	1.♕e5+:♚h6; 2. g5+:♚h5; 3.♗f3+:♝g4; 4.♕h2#	52
#133	1.♕c8+:♕xc8; 2.♗xe5+:♝d6; 3.♖xd6:♝xc2*; 4.♖d7#	53
#134	1. ...:♛b1+; 2.♕e1:♛d3+; 3.♔g1:♛g6+; 4.♔h1*:♛g2#	53
#135	1.♗a7+:♚a8; 2.♗b6+:♚b8; 3.♕a7+:♚c8; 4.♘d6#	53
#136	1.♖dxd5:♜xd5; 2.♖xd5:♛d6; 3.♕xd6:♝xd5*; 4.♕e6#	53
#137	1. ...:h5+; 2.♔h4:♞xf3+; 3.♗xf3: g5+; 4. fxg5 e.p.:♕h3#	54
#138	1.♘xh7+:♜xh7; 2.♕xh7: f5; 3.♖exf5+:♚d8; 4.♖f8# alt: 3. ♖fxf5+:♛ f7; 4.♕xf7# | 2. ...: f6; 3.♖xf6+:♛ f7; 4.♕xf7#	54

?	solutions | soluciones | lösungen | rozwiązania | oplossingen | solvoj	📄
#139	1. ...:♞xc3+; 2.♔b2:♛b1+; 3.♔xc3:♝a5+; 4.b4:♝xb4# alt: 3.♔a3:♛a2+; 4.♔b4:♛a5# | 3.♔a3:♝d6+; 4.b4:♝xb4#	54
#140	1.♖xb7+:♚a8; 2.♖b8+:♚xb8; 3.♖b1+:♚c2; 4.♖b7#	54
#141	1. ...:♝c1+; 2.♖xc1:♜e6; 3.♗d8:♜a6+; 4.♗a5:♜xa5#	55
#142	1.♖e8+:♚d6; 2.♖h6+:♜g6; 3.♖xg6+:♚d7; 4.♗b5#	55
#143	1. ...:♛e2; 2.♛xe2: fxe2; 3.♞d2: e1=♛+; 4.♞f1:♛xf1# alt: 3. h3: e1=♛+; 4.♔h2:♛g1#	55
#144	1.♛xa8+:♚d7; 2.♛xb7+:♚d6; 3.♛c7+:♚d5; 4.bxc3#	55
#145	1. ...:♛xa3+; 2.♔xa3:♜a6+; 3.♔b2:♜a2+; 4.♔b3:♝e6#	56
#146	1.♖a5+: bxa5; 2.♖a6+:♚xa6; 3.♞c5+:♚a7; 4.♛b7#	56
#147	1.♖1d7+:♛xd7; 2.♖xd7+:♚c8; 3.♛xc6+:♚b8; 4.♛b7#	56
#148	1. ...:♝b2+; 2.♖xb2:♛a3+; 3.♖a2:♛xc1+; 4.♗xc1:♜b1#	56
#149	1.♞e7+:♚f8; 2.♞g6+:♚e8; 3.♛e6+:♚e7; 4.♖h8#	57
#150	1.♖c6+:♚xc6; 2.♛a6+:♚c7; 3.♛a7+:♚c6; 4.♗d7# alt: 3. ...:♚d8; 4.♛d7#	57
#151	1.♞f5:♜f7; 2.♖d4:♛e8; 3.♛g7+:♜xg7; 4. fxg7#	57
#152	1. a4+:♚c6; 2.♞a5+:♚d5; 3.♛f7+:♞e6; 4.♖cd1#	57
#153	1.♛h8+:♚e7; 2.♞f5+:♚f6; 3.♛xg7+:♚xf5; 4.♛g5#	58
#154	1. ...:♝xb4+; 2.♖xb4:♛xa2+; 3.♛a3:♛xa3+; 4.♖a4:♛xa4#	58
#155	1.♞d5+:exd5; 2.♗xf6+:♚d6; 3.♗e5+:♚e7; 4.♗d6#	58

♚♛♜♝♞♙ | ♚♛♜♝♞♟

?	solutions | soluciones | lösungen | rozwiązania | oplossingen | solvoj	🖹
#156	1.♜d8+:♝e8; 2.♜xe8+:♚h7; 3.♛xh6+:♚xh6*; 4.♜h8#	58
#157	1.♜c1:♝c5; 2.♛b5+:♝b6; 3.♜c7+:♚a8; 4.♛c6#	59
#158	1. ...:♜a2+; 2.♚xa2:♛a4+; 3.♚b2:♝a3+; 4.♚a1:♝c1#	59
#159	1. ...:♛b2+; 2.♜xb2; d2+; 3.♜c2: d1=♛+:Qc1; 4.♝xc2#	59
#160	1.♝xh7+:♚xh7; 2.♛h5+:♚g8; 3.♜xf8+:♚xf8; 4.♛f7#	59
#161	1.♝b6+:♚d7; 2.♜d3+:♞d6; 3.♜xd6+:♚e7; 4.♜xf7#	60
#162	1. ...:♜xf1+; 2.♚xf1:♜h1+; 3.♜g1:♝xb5+; 4.♚g2:♛h3#	60
#163	1. ...: d3; 2.♝d1:♞xd1; 3.♞xd3:♛xc2+; 4.♚a1:♛a2#	60
#164	1. ...:♞g3+; 2.♚h2:♞f1+; 3.♚h1:♛h2+; 4.♜xh2:♞g2#	60
#165	1.♜xg7:♛d2; 2.♜f3:♜xf3; 3.♜xg8+:♚h7; 4.♜1g7#	61
#166	1. ...:♜xd3+; 2.♞c3:♛d5+; 3.♚a4:♝d7+; 4.♚a5:♛a6#	61
#167	1.♜g8+:♚h7; 2.♝e4+:♚h6; 3.♜h8+:♜h7; 4.♜xh7#	61
#168	1. ...: c3+; 2.♚a1: b2+; 3.♚b1: c2+; 4.♚xb2:♛c3#	61
#169	1. ...:♛a6+; 2.♚c2:♛a4+; 3.♚b1:♛d1+; 4.♞c1:♛xc1#	62
#170	1.♛e8+:♚h7; 2.♝g8+:♚h8; 3.♝f7+:♚h7; 4.♛g8#	62
#171	1.♝xc7+:♚c8; 2.♛a6+:♚d7; 3.♞e5+:♚e6; 4.♞f4#	62
#172	1.♞c6+:♜xc6; 2.♜d8+:♜c8; 3.♜xc8+:♚xc8; 4.♛d8#	62
#173	1. ...:♛c3+; 2.♚a2:♝b3+; 3.♚b1:♛a3+; 4.♚a1:♛a2# alt: 3.♚a3:♝c4+; 4.♚a4:♛a5#	63
#174	1.♝xf6+:♜xf6; 2.♜g4+:♚h7; 3.♛g8+:♚h6; 4.♜h4#	63

?	solutions | soluciones | lösungen | rozwiązania | oplossingen | solvoj	
#175	1.♖b4:♕e1; 2.♖b5+:♔a6; 3.♕xe1;♗d7*; 4.♕a5#	63
#176	1.♖b6+: axb6; 2.♕xb6+:♔e5; 3.♕xc5+:♕d5; 4.♕xd5#	63
#177	1.♕d5+:♔e7; 2.♕f7+:♔d6; 3.♕f8+:♔e6; 4.♕f6#	64
#178	1. ...:♞c2+; 2.♔b1:♞a3+; 3.♔a1:♕b1+; 4.♖xb1:♞c3#	64
#179	1. ...:♗b4+; 2.♔b3:♖a3+; 3.♔b2:♗c3+; 4.♔b1:♖a1#	64
#180	1.♘xe6+:♔e7; 2.♖xg7+:♔xe6; 3.♕e6+:♔xe5; 4. f4#	64
#181	1.♕xc5+:♗c6; 2.♕xd6:♗a4; 3.♖xa4:Nd7; 4.♖a8+:♞b8; 5.♖xb8#	66
#182	1.♕g5+:♔f8; 2.♘g6+:hxg6; 3.♕h6+:♔g8; 4.♖e8+:♖f8; 5.♖xf8#	66
#183	1.♖xh7+:♔g8; 2.♕h5:♗xf2+; 3.♔xf2:♔f8; 4.♖h8+:♗g8; 5.♖xg8#	66
#184	1. ...:♕e7+; 2.♗xe7:♞e6+; 3.♔e1:♖d1+; 4.♗xd1:♞xc2+; 5.♔f1:♖e1#	66
#185	1. ...:♕a3+; 2.♔a1:♕xa2+ 3.♔xa2:♖a6+ 4.♔b2:♗a3+; 5.♔a1:♗xc1#	67
#186	1.♕a4+:♖d7; 2.♕a8+:♖d8; 3.♖xe7+:♔xe7; 4.♕e4+:♔d6; 5.♕e6# alt: 4. ...:♔f6; 5.♕e5#	67
#187	1.♘e7+:♔h8; 2.♕f7:♞f6; 3. e5:♗xe5; 4.♕g8+:♞xg8; 5.♘f6#	67
#188	1.♗xg7+:♔g8; 2.♘h6+:♔xg7; 3.♕g4+:♔xh6; 4.♖h3+:♕h5; 5.♖xh5#	67
#189	1.♖h8+:♔f7; 2.♖xg7+:♔xg7; 3.♕h6+:♔f7; 4.♕f8+:♔g6; 5.♖h6#	68
#190	1. ...:♕e4+; 2.♔b5: a6+; 3.♔xa6:♕d3+; 4. b5:♕a3+; 5.♕xa3:♖xa3#	68

♔♕♖♗♘♙ | ♚♛♜♝♞♟

#	Solution	Page
#191	1.♕xa6+:♚b8; 2.♕xc8+:♔xc8; 3.♖xc7+:♚b8; 4.♖c8+:♚a7; 5.♖1c7	68
#192	1. …:♕f3+; 2.♔g1:♞xf4; 3.♕e4: fxe4; 4. gxf4:♜xh4; 5.♖h5*:♛h1# alt: 5.♔g1:♜h1#	68
#193	1. …:♜h1+; 2.♜c1:♞b4; 3.♗xc7:♚c8; 4.♖xh1:♕a2+; 5.♔c1:♕a1#	69
#194	1.♕xg2+:♚f5; 2.♗h3+:♚xf4 3.♕g5+:♚f3; 4.♕g4+:♚d3; 5.♕d4#	69
#195	1.♗c6+:♚b8; 2.♕xa7+:♚xa7; 3.♖a5+:♚b8; 4.♗xb6:♝d6*; 5.♖a8#	69
#196	1. …:♞d3+; 2.♕xd3:♛h1+; 3.♕f1:♛e4+; 4.♘e3:♛b4+; 5. ♔d1:♛d2#	69
#197	1.♘d5: f6; 2.♗xf6: gxf6; 3.♘g6+:♚g8; 4.♕h8+:♚f7 5.♕h7#	70
#198	1.♘d5+:♚e6; 2.♘d4+:♚xd5; 3.♕b5+:♚xd4; 4. c3+:♚e4; 5.♗d3#	70
#199	1.♗c6: bxc6; 2. bxc6:♚b8; 3.♖ga1:♝a5; 4.♖xa5:♚c8*; 5.♖a8#	70
#200	1. …:♜cd8+; 2.♘5d4:♜xd4+; 3.♕d3:♜xd3+; 4. cxd3:♕xd3+; 5.♔c1:♛c2#	70
#201	1.♖a8+:♝xa8; 2.♕b8+:♝xb8; 3.♖xb6+:♚f7; 4.♖f8+:♚e7; 5.♗g5+:♚d7; 6.♖d8#	72
#202	1. …:♜a8+; 2.♔b3:♝c4+; 3.♔c3:♜c1+; 4.♘xc1:♕xc1+; 5.♔d4: c5+; 6.♗xc5: bxc5#	72
#203	1.♖b7+:♚c1; 2.♖xe7+:♚b1; 3.♖b2+:♚c1; 4.♖xh7+:♚b1; 5.♖xh8+:♛d8; 6.♖xd8#	72

♚♛♜♝♞♟ | ♚♛♜♗♘♙

?	solutions | soluciones | lösungen | rozwiązania | oplossingen | solvoj	📄
#204	1. ....:♛xg4+; 2.♔xg4:♗h5+; 3.♔f5: g6+; 4.♔e6:♗g4+; 5. ♔d5:♜b5+; 6.♔c4:♞d6#	72
#205	1. b5+:♔a5; 2.♘c6+:♜xc6; 3.♔b3:♜xc4; 4.♔xc4: a6; 5.♜a7: h1=♛*; 6.♜xa6#	73
#206	1.♜b8+:♚a7; 2.♗c5+:♚a6; 3. c8=♛+:♛xc8; 4.♗xc8+:♚a5; 5.♜a8+:♚b5; 6.♜b2#	73
#207	1. ....:♜a1+; 2.♔xa1:♜a5+; 3.♔b1:♜a1+; 4.♔xa1:♛a8+; 5.♔b1:♛a2+; 6.♔c1:♛a1#	73
#208	1.♔b6:♚c8; 2.♜c7+:♚b8; 3.♜d7:♗f5; 4.♜d8:♗c8; 5.♗e5+:♚a8; 6.♜xc8# alt 3. ....:♜c3; 4.♜d8+:♜c8; 5.♗e5+:♚a8; 6.♜xc8#	73

Acknowledgments | Remerciements | Agradecimientos
Danksagungen | Podziękowania | Dankbetuigingen | Dankoj

This book was created with the following free software products:
Ce livre a été créé à l'aide des logiciels gratuits suivants:
Este libro fue creado utilizando los siguientes productos de software libre:
Dieses Buch wurde mit den folgenden freien Softwareprodukten erstellt:
Ta książka została utworzona przy użyciu następujących bezpłatnych produktów oprogramowania:
Dit boek is gemaakt met de volgende gratis softwareproducten:
Ĉi tiu libro estis kreita kun la jenaj liberaj programoj:

SCID – Shane's Chess
Information Database
http://scid.sourceforge.net/

GIMP – GNU Image
Manipulation Program
https://gimp.org/

LibreOffice –
The Document Foundation
https://www.libreoffice.org/

**Dziękuję! Bedankt! ¡Gracias!
Thank You! Dankon! Merci! Danke!**

QR - FEN

Nº 1	Nº 2	Nº 3	Nº 4	Nº 5	Nº 6
Nº 7	Nº 8	Nº 9	Nº 10	Nº 11	Nº 12
Nº 13	Nº 14	Nº 15	Nº 16	Nº17	Nº 18
Nº 19	Nº 20	Nº 21	Nº 22	Nº 23	Nº 24
Nº 25	Nº 26	Nº 27	Nº 28	Nº 29	Nº 30

QR - FEN

Nº 31   Nº 32   Nº 33   Nº 34   Nº 35   Nº 36

Nº 37   Nº 38   Nº 39   Nº 40   Nº 41   Nº 42

Nº 43   Nº 44   Nº 45   Nº 46   Nº 47   Nº 48

Nº 49   Nº 50   Nº 51   Nº 52   Nº 53   Nº 54

Nº 55   Nº 56   Nº 57   Nº 58   Nº 59   Nº 60

QR - FEN

Nº 61   Nº 62   Nº 63   Nº 64   Nº 65   Nº 66

Nº 67   Nº 68   Nº 69   Nº 70   Nº 71   Nº 72

Nº 73   Nº 74   Nº 75   Nº 76   Nº 77   Nº 78

Nº 79   Nº 80   Nº 81   Nº 82   Nº 83   Nº 84

Nº 85   Nº 86   Nº 87   Nº 88   Nº 89   Nº 90

QR - FEN

Nº 91   Nº 92   Nº 93   Nº 94   Nº 95   Nº 96

Nº 97   Nº 98   Nº 99   Nº 100   Nº 101   Nº 102

Nº 103   Nº 104   Nº 105   Nº 106   Nº 107   Nº 108

Nº 109   Nº 110   Nº 111   Nº 112   Nº 113   Nº 114

Nº 115   Nº 116   Nº 117   Nº 118   Nº 119   Nº 120

QR - FEN

Nº 121   Nº 122   Nº 123   Nº 124   Nº 125   Nº 126

Nº 127   Nº 128   Nº 129   Nº 130   Nº 131   Nº 132

Nº 133   Nº 134   Nº 135   Nº 136   Nº 137   Nº 138

Nº 139   Nº 140   Nº 141   Nº 142   Nº 143   Nº 144

Nº 145   Nº 146   Nº 147   Nº 148   Nº 149   Nº 150

QR - FEN

Nº 151	Nº 152	Nº 153	Nº 154	Nº 155	Nº 156
Nº 157	Nº 158	Nº 159	Nº 160	Nº 161	Nº 162
Nº 163	Nº 164	Nº 165	Nº 166	Nº 167	Nº 168
Nº 169	Nº 170	Nº 171	Nº 172	Nº 173	Nº 174
Nº 175	Nº 176	Nº 177	Nº 178	Nº 179	Nº 180

QR - FEN

Nº 181 Nº 182 Nº 183 Nº 184 Nº 185 Nº 186

Nº 187 Nº 188 Nº 189 Nº 190 Nº 191 Nº 192

Nº 193 Nº 194 Nº 195 Nº 196 Nº 137 Nº 198

Nº 199 Nº 200 Nº 201 Nº 202 Nº 203 Nº 204

Nº 205 Nº 206 Nº 207 Nº 208

Bildernachweis:
Alle Grafiken wurden vom Autor erstellt. Das Cover basiert auf einem Foto von George Becker unter der pexels-Lizenz: https://www.pexels.com/photo/12 9742/